The Vermilion County Museum Society is pleased to release the second printing of the very popular *Danville: A Pictorial History*. We want to extend our appreciation to the Board of Directors, officers and employees of the First National Bank of Danville for displaying their commendable concern for local history by sponsoring the Limited Edition of *Danville: A Pictorial History* in 1987. Their successful efforts in this project provides an inspiring example of the positive benefits of preserving the heritage of our fine community.

# BOB WRIGHT
May 20, 1916 - July 7, 1988

*From column by Kevin Cullen,
Commercial-News, July 7, 1988*

Danville lost one of its best friends this morning.

Robert B. "Bob" Wright, who chronicled Danville's past and present in the pages of the *Commercial-News* for nearly 50 years, died at 4:20 a.m.

A gifted, respected and beloved writer, Wright was perhaps best known for his reflections on local history, current events and life's eternal verities. His editorials and his columns won several awards.

Wright was among a few Danville men who helped save the Dr. William Fithian home from demolition in the early 1960s. That house is now the Vermilion County Museum.

Wright helped found the Danville Jaycees, the Vermilion County Museum Society and the Danville Humane Society. He was active in the Red Mask Players for nearly 50 years, served three years on the Danville Library Board and was former chairman of the Salvation Army Board.

"Bob was a historical anchor," said John Sanders ... "The most wonderful thing about him was that he walked, and felt, and heard the streets of Danville, and was able to give all of us a sense of living history."

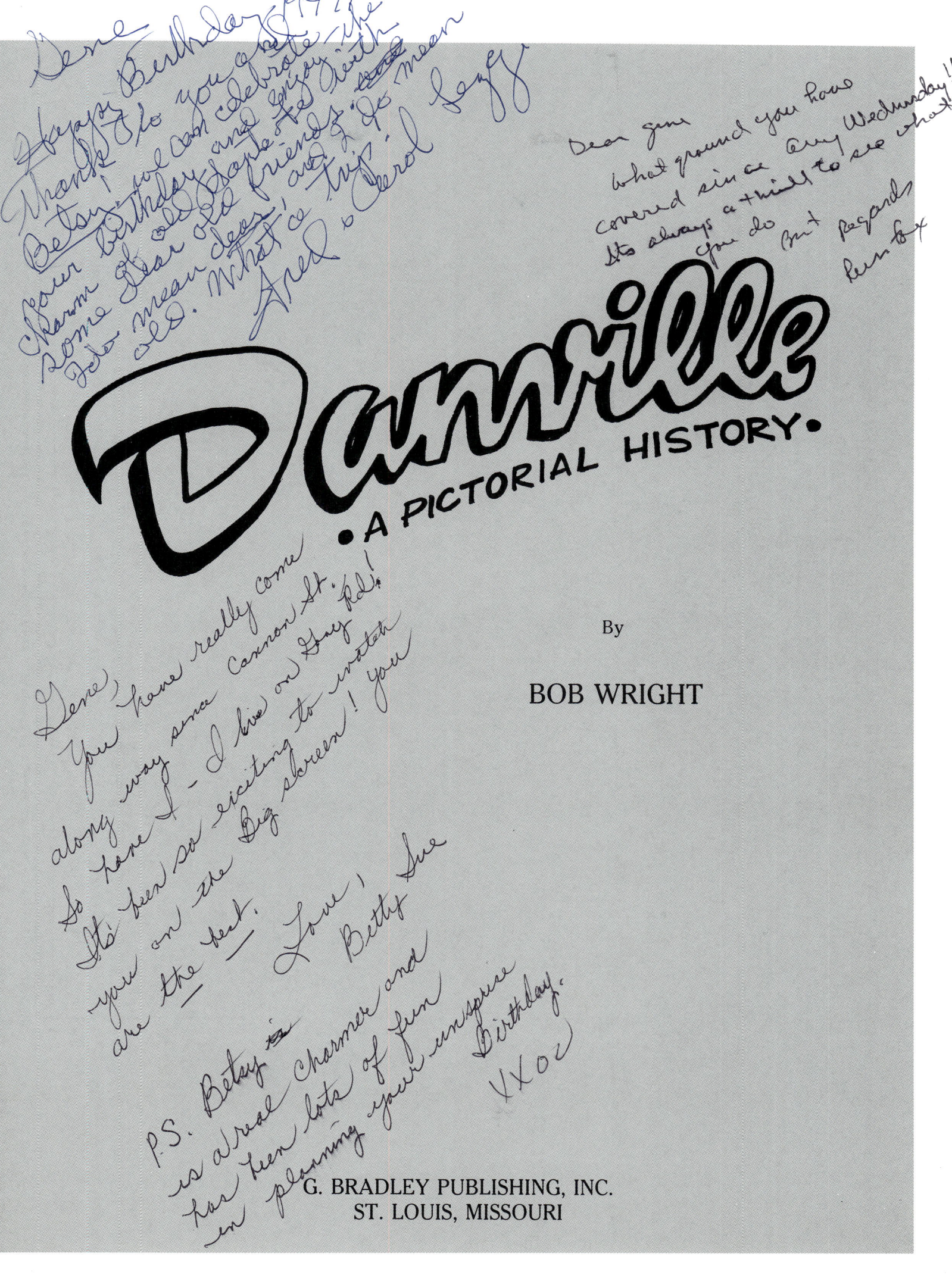

# DANVILLE

**A PICTORIAL HISTORY**
By
Bob Wright

PUBLICATION STAFF
  AUTHOR: Bob Wright
  FOREWORD: Kevin Cullen
  HISTORIC SKETCHES: Frank "Bud" Cullen
  BOOK DESIGN: IPC Graphics
  PUBLISHER: G. Bradley Publishing, Inc.
  SPONSOR: Vermilion County Museum Society

Photographs not specifically identified are from the Vermillion County Museum, the Commercial-News and the author's personal collection.

Majority of Chapter V photographs are courtesy of Rich Stefaniak and Chuck Cannady.

First Edition 1987
Second Printing 1988

Copyright 1987 by G. Bradley Publishing, Inc. All Rights Reserved. Printed in the United States of America. No part of this publication may be reproduced, stored in a retrieval system, or transmitted, in any form or by any means, electronic, mechanical, photocopying, recording, or otherwise, without the prior written permission of the publisher.

ISBN 0-943963-01-X
Printed in the United States of America

# TABLE OF CONTENTS

Foreword . . . . . . . . . . . . . . . . . . . . . . . . . . . . . . . . . . . . . . . . . . 7

Chapter I: Salt to Settlement 1819 - 1860 . . . . . . . . . . . . . . . . . . . 9

Chapter II: War and Peace 1861 - 1890 . . . . . . . . . . . . . . . . . . . . 29

Chapter III: More Wars and Growth 1891 - 1920 . . . . . . . . . . . . . . 65

Chapter IV: Boom, Bust and Battle 1921 - 1950 . . . . . . . . . . . . . . 127

Chapter V: Recovery and Change 1951 - Present . . . . . . . . . . . . . 169

Acknowledgments . . . . . . . . . . . . . . . . . . . . . . . . . . . . . . . 196

Bibliography . . . . . . . . . . . . . . . . . . . . . . . . . . . . . . . . . . . 197

Index . . . . . . . . . . . . . . . . . . . . . . . . . . . . . . . . . . . . . . . 198

# FOREWORD

If a picture is worth a thousand words, the truest history lies in photographs. Fragile emulsions capture the past unwashed, unedited and unabridged.

Through photography, we experience scenes and people that our great-great-grandfathers saw. The same lights and shadows, the same pits and pimples. The photos connect, in a magical, personal way, "then" with "now."

This book, written and edited by Danville newspaperman and historian Bob Wright, uses images to present the story of Danville, Vermilion County, Illinois. As you turn the pages, you will see that there have been many Danvilles, each distinct, yet each lending itself to the city we see today.

We long for a glimpse of the earliest days, lived before photography was born. The frontier town, platted in 1826-27, stood on the site of a Piankeshaw Indian village. History speaks of majestic sandstone bluffs overlooking the Vermilion River downtown, bluffs later quarried for bridge abutments. Gone are the wild grapes and virgin forests, prairie grasses and passenger pigeons.

Frontier life was hard and mean. The village consisted of a few log cabins, a wood-frame trading post, a county courthouse and streets forever shifting from mud to dust to mud again. Gurdon Hubbard, Dan Beckwith, Amos Williams, Solomon Gilbert and Seymour Treat formed and guided the fledgling hamlet.

The first two decades of our municipal existence live only in the imagination of artists. But after 1850, photographers and their unwieldy equipment captured the passing of a town and the birth of a city.

Through the images they captured, we can see, for example, the McCormack House, where Lincoln boarded; the Vermilion County Courthouse of 1832, where he practiced law while riding the Eighth Judicial Circuit. We see the virile, handsome face of Ward Hill Lamon, with whom Lincoln shared a law office on the public square.

Flip a few more pages and we see "another" Danville, 50 years later. The old landmarks, the old settlers, have given way. Railroads, coal mining, farming and heavy industry have changed all. The age of steam and steel is at full throttle. Danville is feeling its oats, proud of itself, confident of the future. Germans, Swedes and Irish struggle and prosper. The local congressman, Joe Cannon, is speaker of the House. Civic boosters organize the "100,000 Club."

We see iron-jawed leaders with handle-bar mustaches. We see impressive new buildings rise up—Washington School, the courthouse, the federal building, Elks Club, Danville Public Library. We step inside the showplaces of Roselawn and the humble cottages of Rabbittown and Germantown; we work with miners and field hands and shop keepers. We walk among white-haired veterans of the Civil War at Danville's Soldiers Home.

Finally, we see familiar images of Danville today. It is a city in transition, struggling to understand the past, often ignoring its lessons. Landmarks vanish, and others take their place; men and women play their part, then pass from view. Once-important industries and neighborhoods dwindle and die, to be replaced by new, different upstarts.

Such is the story of our town. We hope that you find—by viewing the slices of past realities pressed between these covers—a keener appreciation of the present and hope for the future.

—KEVIN CULLEN

## AMOS WILLIAMS

"A jack of all trades" probably would be one of the best ways to describe Danville's leading pioneer citizen, Amos Williams. But the remainder of the familiar saying would have to be amended to: "Master of many."

For the most part, Williams WAS Danville during the town's formative years. There was scarcely an activity, official or otherwise, in which he was not involved.

His education was extensive, especially when compared with that of his neighbors. He was a fluent and artistic writer, learned the printing trade during his youthful indenture, and was familiar with the tools of the surveyor.

In Pennsylvania, where he was born in 1797, he served an apprenticeship with a Chambersburg printer. And when he went to work for the Dutch newspaper, he became proficient in that language.

The urge to see more of the country led to his leaving the East when he was 21. Before reaching Danville, he helped organize Edgar County, did some surveying there and taught school. It was here that he was married in 1826 to Martha Ann Shaw.

Williams' accomplishments in Edgar County were just a preview of what was to come in Vermilion. In the 30 years he lived here, he held more public offices than any other man in local history.

He began by helping to organize the county when he came here in 1826. Appointed the first postmaster the same year, he was instrumental in moving the county seat from its provisional location, Butler's Point (near present-day Catlin) to Danville.

Williams apparently thought Vermilion County showed promise. He erected a house, the first to be built in the soon-to-be-formed city, in 1827 and then, as newly-appointed county agent, conducted the first sale of lots in Danville in April of that year.

Hitching up a covered wagon, he returned to the East to bring his mother and younger sister to the new town.

As postmaster, Williams had discovered that mail destined for Vermilion County sometimes wound up in Vermillion County, Indiana. And so he urged naming the community Danville for his friend and brother-in-law, Dan Beckwith, who had given land for the town site.

In the following years, his other official duties included recorder of deeds, judge of probate court, notary public, registrar of saline lands and master in chancery.

In addition to these tasks, he was active in church and school affairs. He provided a building on his own land for a school (at 124 Franklin Street, present site of the Christian Home for Youth).

Williams had enough experience with horse and wagon travel to know the importance of better transportation. His 1827 trip to Pennsylvania had taken eight weeks each way. He joined a group of men meeting to arouse interest in a railroad called the Northern Cross, a line which eventually was routed through Danville.

Williams' business acumen showed through in later years. The mills he built and operated helped the growing city's economy.

He died on November 14, 1857.

## DAN BECKWITH

No likeness exists of Dan Beckwith, inasmuch as he lived before the development of photography and no artist sketched him. We know that he was born in Pennsylvania in 1795, that he came to Indiana as a young man, settling near Fort Harrison (in what is now the Terre Haute area) and that he was interested in the "salines of the Vermilion," and accompanied the first white explorers to the site.

From accounts of his contemporaries, we deduce that he probably was a six-footer, strongly built, an expert axe-man and woodsman. He surveyed the Danville townsite and assisted Amos Williams, his brother-in-law, in drawing up the town's original plat. He had donated 20 acres for the county seat-to-be and a contemporary, Guy Smith, contributed another 80 acres. Beckwith thought the new community should be named "Williamstown" or "Williamsburg" but his brother-in-law's counter-suggestion of "Danville" prevailed with the first county commissioners.

Danville's namesake, who operated a trading post at the west end of Main Street, had business in Washington in December, 1835. It was while returning from there on horseback that he contracted pneumonia. He died on Christmas Day at age 40.

The accompanying sketch, by Frank "Bud" Cullen, is the Danville historical artist's conception of what Dan Beckwith probably looked like in the prime of life.

## FIRST INDUSTRY

*Hi Gene*

*I remember many things we did together. We weren't angels but we never did anything that bad. I remember dating, playing ping-pong and all the things that didn't cost money. You have given me many happy moments. After all is said and done the most important things in life are health and happiness. I hope you have both.*

*Your friend*
*Don Lucas*

These huge kettles (each had a capacity of 140 gallons of brine) represent Danville's first industry. One hundred gallons boiled down produced a bushel of salt. Settlers from all over Illinois and nearby Indiana came on horseback or driving slow-moving oxen teams to buy the product at $1.25 to $1.50 per bushel.

# CHAPTER I

# SALT TO SETTLEMENT

## 1819 - 1860

Quite legitimately, Danville could adopt as its motto, "Salt of the earth." For quite literally, this community owes its beginning to salt.

Back in the 16th century, nearly 400 years ago, the Vermilion River was known to the French. And the "Salines of the Vermilion" are referred to in French records as early as 1706.

Again in 1750, there is reference to these "salines," or flowing salt springs, in the records of the Jesuit Fathers in Montreal. The intrepid priests visited the "salines" in that year and found the "largest Indian village within a six-day journey," or about 120 miles. It was a village of the Kickapoos and extended from a point west of the "salines" to within six to eight miles of where the Vermilion empties into the Wabash River east of present-day Cayuga, Indiana. It occupied both sides of the river and the natives showed an advanced state of civilization. Some had rude cabins instead of wigwams. And there were patches of pumpkins and corn, enclosed with brush fences, indicating individual ownership.

This was the beginning of the white man's intrusion into what had been the Indians' private domain. Joseph Barron, who was William Henry Harrison's interpreter in dealings with the Indians, first visited the "salines" in 1801 but found the area unoccupied, with signs of human habitation reverting to nature. But Barron saw the economic possibilities of the area and returned with a party of other frontiersmen on September 22, 1819. The date is significant; the white man had come to stay. A member of that party, Seymour Treat, brought his wife and children from Fort Harrison (located near what is now Terre Haute, Indiana), traveling up the Wabash and Vermilion Rivers in a *pirogue* (a canoe made by hollowing out a large log). Soon, the little family had settled in as Danville's first permanent residents.

But although salt-making, which evolved from those early 19th century explorations, became an industry, it had lived its life by 1840.

So what brought Danville to life? And what kept it alive?

The answer is trade — trade with the Indians at first, then ever-expanding trade with the white settlers. Men like Dan Beckwith and Gurdon Hubbard who operated trading posts were the first successful businessmen; men like Seymour Treat and Amos Williams who built sawmills and grist mills were the entrepreneurs, the risk takers, without whom no community can grow.

Beckwith's first mercantile venture, according to his historian son, Hiram, was ". . . an armful of goods suitable for Indian barter, which he kept in a place partly excavated in a side of the hill at Denmark, as early, probably, as the year 1821." The village of Denmark was short-lived and the site is now covered by the waters of Lake Vermilion. Subsequently, he built a log hut on the brow of the hill above present-day Ellsworth Park, where W. Main Street begins its slope down to the highway bridge across the North Fork River. His next storeroom was just west of the elm tree (the old Council Elm) on the North Fork river bank.

Hubbard established a much larger trade with the Indians. According to Hiram Beckwith, he ". . . followed the Indians in their hunting rounds, and in this way acquired an early knowledge of all the country between the Wabash and Illinois rivers, as far north as Chicago and as far south as Vincennes. As the 22-year-old head of the American Fur Company's Illinois operations, he abandoned the posts on the Illinois River and introduced pack-horses in place of boats, using the "Hubbard's Trace," as his trail from Chicago to the salt works was called, to conduct the fur trade. In 1827 he abandoned the posts on the Embarrass and Little Wabash rivers and constructed his trading post in Danville.

For a few years, Hubbard's fur trade with the Indians was brisk. Beckwith has this commentary in his "History of Vermilion County": "The Indians would file into town on their ponies, sometimes 50 or a hundred, with their furs, squaws and papooses, when trade at Hubbard's corner would be unusually lively for a few days. The Indians would camp on the bluff east of Walnut street or farther down toward the (later site of) the railway bridge, where they would enjoy themselves and feast on bread made out of flour, and upon meat and other luxuries, for which they had exchanged their furs . . . In 1832, the fur trade having declined on account of the scarcity of fur-bearing animals in, and the dispersion of the Indians from this section of country, Col. Hubbard converted his stock into white goods — as merchandise suitable for white people were called to distinguish them from the kind adapted to the Indian trade. During the same year, he sold out his stock to Dr. (W.E.) Fithian and in 1833 took up his permanent residence in Chicago." It is interesting to note that today's "white sales," referring to bed sheets and linens, had an earlier and quite different meaning.

History is vague as to the power source of the first mills in and around Danville. Some were operated by mill hands, using the strength of muscular backs and arms to turn the heavy millstones, burred to grind the corn and wheat. Others were operated by water; in such instances, the North Fork was dammed and a flume extended above the mill wheel, a drop of six feet was considered sufficient to turn the wheel in a consistent, steady revolution to supply power. Seymour Treat was one of the first mill owners; he left the salt works in 1832 and built a substantial home in the village of Denmark, where he set up the first sawmill. His home doubled as a tavern (hotel) for many years and was the last structure razed before the site of the long-abandoned village was covered by the waters of Lake Vermilion in 1925.

Amos Williams built a mill on the North Fork, probably around 1836. Robert Kirkpatrick built a water mill on Stony Creek a year earlier and ran it as a sawmill for several years.

So many mills were in operation along the North Fork, north from its confluence with the Salt Fork, that the street on the bluff above it was Mill Street until being renamed for Illinois' Civil War hero, Gen. John A. Logan. In later years, most mills were powered by steam and the principal product was flour.

But despite business development, Danville grew slowly. In 1855, with no railroad, the population had reached only 1,125.

Then, all of a sudden, two things happened in the late 1850s that were to affect Danville's future profoundly.

The first of these was completion of the Great Western Railroad into the city in 1856. In a matter of a few years, the population of the city had reached 2,000.

It must be kept in mind that in the early days, Danville merchants had to take their products to river towns and haul all merchandise and other commodities back. Says Historian Beckwith: "The whole country as far west as the Sangamon River was thus made tributary to and wholly dependent on the (Indian towns of) LaFayette, Attica, Covington, Perrysville, Eugene and Clinton for their supplies. It was not until after the modern system of transportation by railroads was successfully inaugurated that we were released from our bondage to the Wabash River or the canal running alongside of it."

In 1835, a charter was obtained for the Chicago & Vincennes Railway (to connect the two cities by way of Danville) and in the same year a charter was secured for a railroad for Quincy, Illinois, to the Indiana state line in the direction of LaFayette, via Springfield, Decatur and Danville under the name of the "Northern Cross Railroad." This became the Great Western and ultimately the Wabash and the Norfolk & Southern.

Danville's Dr. William E. Fithian was a member of the Illinois legislature at the time and shrewdly wrote into the appropriation bill a proviso that work should begin in Vermilion County. A financial crisis soon stopped the work but when construction was resumed, what had been done was too valuable to waste.

The second growth factor was the beginning of coal mining operations around 1857. As these expanded, along with railroad service, trade also grew to serve the enlarging agricultural area.

---

CHIEF KEANNEKEUK

Chief *Keannekeuk* (pronounced Kee-an-uh-kee-uhk) was the first effective temperance leader in Vermilion County.

The August, 1831, edition of the *Illinois Monthly* magazine, published at Vandalia, observed: "It is proper to remark that *Keannekeuk* was at one time given to being intemperate. About four years since, he reformed, and is now esteemed a correct, pious and excellent man. He has acquired an astonishing influence over the red brethren and has induced all of his particular tribe, supposed to be near 200, and about 100 Potawatomies who have been inveterate drunkards, to abstain entirely from the use of ardent spirits. It is proper further to

UNDER THE COUNCIL ELM

Chief *Keannekeuk*, on horseback, exhorts his tribe to abstain from drinking whiskey and to follow religious ways. The Council Elm in Ellsworth Park thrived well into the 20th century; its site today is marked by an appropriate monument erected during the nation's Bicentennial celebration. The chief, whose name's spelling has been corrupted, is honored today by Kennekuk Cove County Park, west of Danville.

remark that *Keannekeuk* is called a prophet among the Indians, but is not the old prophet, brother to *Tecumseh*, who is known to be not less odious among the Indians than among the whites, nor is he related to him. *Keannekeuk* appears to be about 40 years of age (he actually was 34 at the time), is over the ordinary size, and although an untutored savage, has much in his manner and personal appearance to make him interesting . . ."

George Catlin, regarded as the foremost painter of early Indian life, produced the portrait from which the accompanying photograph was made. The original today is a part of the National Collection of Fine Arts of the Smithsonian Institute in Washington, D.C.

By treaty with the U.S. government, the Kickapoos gave up their land around Danville in 1834 and were moved to a reservation in Kansas. *Keannekeuk* went with them and remained as their chief until his death in 1853.

## ORIGINAL PLAT

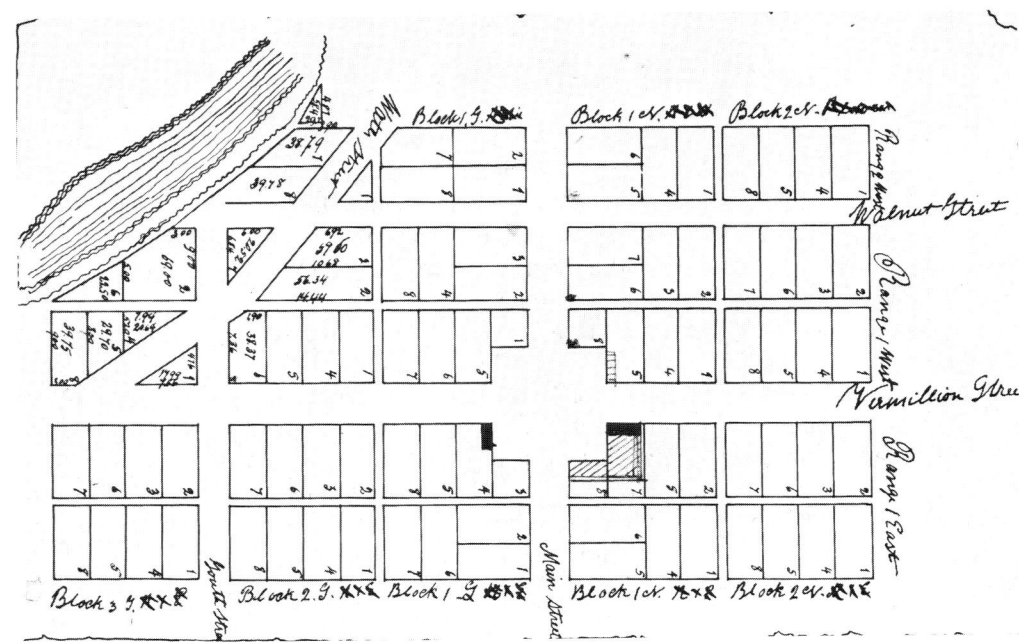

This is a copy of the first plat of Danville drawn by Dan Beckwith, surveyor, and Amos Williams in April, 1827. Only five streets are named: Water, South, Main, Vermilion and Walnut. Cross streets of Main led to the Vermilion River; it was hoped that the city would become a port. Black area, east side of Vermilion Street on the north side of the square, marks the location of the first permanent courthouse. Other shadings in grey indicate expansion to the present site of the building. The first courthouse in Danville, a log structure, faced the square on the new Palmer-American Bank site.

## RATTLESNAKE SCARE

It was a warm April 10, Danville's birthday in 1827, and a crowd had assembled for the first sale of lots in the new county seat of Vermilion County.

The event had been advertised well in the *Illinois Intelligencer* at Vandalia and in the Indianapolis, Indiana, newspaper.

But the chant of auctioneer Harvey Luddington had to compete with the whinnying of tethered horses. So proceedings were halted temporarily for investigation.

It was the snare-drum shuffle clicking of rattlesnakes that was frightening the horses. An impromptu hunt began immediately, with the would-be lot purchasers armed with clubs. Some 75 to 80 rattlers, many six feet long, were killed and scores more were driven back to their dens in the rock ledges above the nearby Vermilion River before the sale was resumed.

Despite the bizarre adjournment, the sale went well. Amos Williams, a man who held almost every position of authority in Danville at one time or another, acted as agent. His report showed that 42 lots had been sold, and the total amount realized was $992.87. This made the average price not quite $22. The site of today's First National Bank drive-in banking complex went for $17. The lot upon which Gurdon Hubbard built his trading post was the most expensive: $37.75.

## HORSE-POWERED FERRY

No one today can be certain just how the early-day ferry was drawn back and forth across the Vermilion River between what is now South Danville and the city proper. This artist's sketch conjectures a practical possibility: Horses on either bank pulling cables which wrapped around millstones, thus pulling the boat back and forth. Use of the ferry was abandoned in 1857, when the covered Red Bridge was built.

George Haworth, one of Danville's pioneers, also was this community's first patron of education. He donated the use of a building he had erected west and north of his hotel as a school — his smokehouse!

Haworth's hostelry was an imposing building for 1827. Built of logs, it was two stories high and contained four rooms. A well was dug and it was made known that the structure was available to Danville residents in the event of an Indian attack.

It faced east on what is now Vermilion Street, approximately in the location of the ell-shaped parking space adjacent to Bresee Tower and the Courthouse Annex. The smokehouse probably was about where that section of the annex which opens onto W. Main Street is located now.

Also made of logs was the makeshift school, which measured 10-by-15 feet and had a dirt floor. Classes were conducted with the smoked meat hanging overhead. Eight or 10 children were enrolled under the tutelage of Dr. Norton Beckwith.

The arrangement was temporary. The improvised schoolhouse was burned, according to the Amos Williams Scrapbook, "by a group of mischievous men." It seems that a Henry Blunt had stored venison hams in the building, intending to ship them to New Orleans by flatboat. While several of the frontier practical jokers distracted Blunt at a grocery, their companions touched off the smokehouse. It may have been hugely amusing at the time but it created something of an educational crisis.

FIRST SCHOOL

PIONEER POST OFFICE

The frame building at left was built in 1826 on S. Clark Street (running south from Main Street west of Walnut, now no longer in existence) and housed Danville's first post office for 20 years. It also was the home of the postmaster, Amos Williams, who resided there until his death in 1857.

## GURDON HUBBARD

Gurdon Saltonstall Hubbard was, in Illinois, what Davey Crockett was in Tennessee.

Once described by a member of the Chicago Literary Society as "the greatest citizen Chicago has ever known," he also ranks as one of Danville's greatest pioneers.

Hubbard, a native of Vermont, came to what was then the Northest in 1818 as a $125-a-year clerk for the American Fur Company. He was just 16 years old.

Ten years later, he had bought out the entire Illinois unit of the Astor Company and was known throughout the state. He then was making his home in Danville.

Already he had established an awesome reputation as a woodsman.

According to Earle Astor Shilton in his book, *Pa-Pa-Ma-Ta-Be*, young Hubbard (he was 21 at the time) "was on a stroll from the vicinity of 'Big Woods' on the Fox River, some 40 miles west of present-day Chicago, to his Bureau Station camp, when he became aware that he was being paced by a young warrior of the Big Foot tribe . . . He had spent the night at a Pottawatomie village with friendly Indians and was unaware that one tribe had bet all its wampum to the effect that one of the Indian lads could walk further and faster in a given day than the white guest."

To make a long story short, Hubbard walked and trotted 75 miles by nightfall, climaxing the feat by swimming the Illinois River. His opponent had dropped out of the race exhausted. The admiring Indians dubbed the young white man "Swift Walker" (*Pa-Pa-Ma-Ta-Be*, in their language), a nickname that was to stick the rest of his life.

He remained popular with the Indians and was married briefly to an Indian princess, whose name, *Watch-e-kee*, survives today in the city Watseka, county seat of Iroquois County.

When the fur business started to decline, he began hauling produce and pork to the garrison of Fort Dearborn and the growing village around it. The route he followed became known as the Hubbard Trace.

It was while residing in Danville that Hubbard performed his greatest feat. He was in Chicago in 1827 on business during the Winnebago War when word came from friendly Indians that an attack on the fort was imminent. He offered to ride to Danville and raise the Vermilion County militia battalion.

He arose from a sickbed and left Chicago on horseback at 4 p.m. in the rain. By midnight he had covered the 80 miles to his Iroquois post, where he obtained food and a remount. A storm-swollen creek forced him to wait until daybreak when he resumed his epic ride. He shouted his news at Denmark (now covered by the waters of Lake Vermilion) and at Danville, then rode two miles farther to another settlement. He had covered 140 miles in 20 hours.

The next day, Hubbard, with 50 armed men on horseback, started out to Chicago's rescue. It took four days to make the trip. On arrival, he was made captain of defense. But the anticipated attack failed to materialize; in a day or two word came from Gov. Cass that the war was over.

In 1834, Hubbard moved permanently to what he described as "that smaller town up on the lake" and for most of the next 52 years of his life he was identified with almost every progressive action of the growing city.

He built the city's first warehouse. With two partners he formed a trading company and established a line of lake streamers serving Buffalo and the upper Great Lakes.

Gurdon Hubbard built this trading post on the southeast corner of the public square about 1828. It was Danville's first frame building; lumber and timbers in it came from Seymour Treat's Denmark sawmill. "Time has shown that it was very substantially built," wrote historian Hiram Beckwith, and this photograph, at left, taken many years later, confirms the appraisal. Palmer-American National Bank occupied the site for many years before building the present structure, a few hundred feet to the west on Main Street. The other structure pictured was Hubbard's home. Located just south of his trading post on what is now Redden Square, it was numbered as 25 S. Vermilion Street. This photo, taken about 1850, does not show the original dimensions; the house extended from the chimney to the extreme left corner of the photograph. Hubbard moved to Chicago in 1834. *Photo courtesy of the Chicago Historical Society.*

## KYGER MILL

This was the Kyger Mill on the Vermilion River, a few miles southeast of Danville near the village of Grape Creek. It was built in 1835 by William Sheets, a leading citizen of nearby Georgetown, and a Thomas Morgan. Its function is obscure; said historian Beckwith in 1879: "After Mr. Kyger came into possession of it, he built a large frame and got in new machinery but has never yet got it running." From this early photograph, it may be reasonably deduced that a dam was intended so that the resulting fall of water could operate the mill wheel. This was a common source of power on the North Fork in Danville, although later mills were operated by steam engines.

## FIRST SPAN

The "Old Red Bridge" was the first to carry a roadway between Danville and South Danville over the Vermilion River. Prior to its construction in 1857, traffic had to ferry the stream. The view in this photo is to the south. The bridge was built at something of a northwest-to-southeast angle, probably to take advantage of the shortest natural distance. Succeeding spans were erected a little to the east and more in line with South Danville hill. It was atop that hill, incidentally, that stagecoaches from the south halted to allow the driver to blow a conch horn, alerting the postmaster in Danville to the imminent arrival of the mail.

## DISTINGUISHED SON

Hiram Beckwith was only three years old when his father, Dan Beckwith, founder of Danville, died. He grew up to study law with Ward Hill Lamon, Lincoln's law partner, and joined them and other luminaries, including Stephen A. Douglas, in law suits on the old Eighth Judicial Circuit. He was a successful businessman but he is remembered chiefly for his interest in history. When the Vermilion County Historical Society was organized in 1877, he became one of the managers. He was the first president of the Illinois State Historical Society and his "History of Vermilion County," written in 1879, is considered by historians as the authority for this area. He also authored histories of Iroquois County (Illinois) and the Indiana counties of Vigo, Parke, Fountain and Montgomery. He died in 1903 at the age of 71.

## NEWELL'S FLYING MACHINE

It was an autumn day in 1841. The chattering crowd on the commons at Newtown, a few miles west of Danville, was in a holiday mood.

They had assembled prepared to jeer what was about to take place. But curiosity had drawn the skeptics like a magnet. Suppose "Crazy Hugh" Newell's stunt should prove not so outlandish after all!

As the great moment approached, the onlookers became quiet. All eyes were on a large haystack atop which rested a contraption like nothing anyone had seen before. A man climbed into it, gave a signal. Willing hands shoved the machine over the edge. There was a frantic flapping of wing-like appendages in the split second before the craft hit the ground and was smashed. Legend has it that it was "Crazy Hugh" himself at the controls and that he crawled from the wreckage with only a broken arm; no clear account exists nearly a century-and-a-half later.

But it is certain that another of man's efforts to fly like a bird was as shattered as the broken machine at the foot of the haystack. Hugh Newell didn't even bother to pick up the pieces.

John and Lawrence T. Allen Jr., prominent Danville lawyers into the 1970s and '80s, now deceased, were Hugh Newell's great-great-grandsons.

## FIRST CHURCH

The First Presbyterian Church, established March 8, 1829, not only was Danville's first church but this frame building, built in 1835, was the first church edifice. It stood on the northwest corner of North and Franklin Streets (site of the present church) before being moved in 1858 to the west side of S. Walnut Street, where the David S. Palmer Civic Center is now located. It served several purposes for many years; as a church, a school and even as a post office when the pastor, the Rev. Enoch Kingsbury, was postmaster. The church was built with folding doors that could be thrown into one or two rooms as needed.

## SECOND COURTHOUSE

Danville's first courthouse was a log cabin on the south side of W. Main Street just west of what is now Towne Centre. Construction of the second courthouse building, pictured here, was begun in 1832 and it was opened for business the following year on the site of the present courthouse. Besides Lincoln, such famed individuals as Edward Baker, Adlai Stevenson I and Daniel W. Voorhees appeared in court in this building. It was destroyed by fire in 1872 but the jail (smaller building to the left) "absolutely refused to follow suit," in the whimsical words of a newspaper account.

## McCORMACK HOUSE

A circuit-riding lawyer who signed the register, "A. Lincoln, Springfield," was the most famous guest of the McCormack House, located on the north side of W. Main Street. The L-shaped building, which extended north paralleling alley, was situated just west of the present-day drive-in complex of First National Bank.

# ABE LINCOLN IN DANVILLE

This could be the title of the real-life drama that had its setting between the years 1841 and 1861. For it was in Danville, during the two decades preceding the Civil War, that Abraham Lincoln spent much of his time.

Although a resident of Springfield, the gangling young country lawyer was a familiar figure on Danville streets as he passed the time of day with friends and acquaintances between sessions of court, which was on the old Eighth Judicial Circuit. (Parenthetically, to be a circuit-riding lawyer in those days required a great deal of time in addition to unusual stamina; the district embraced some 13,000 square miles or very nearly one-quarter of the state's area.)

The earliest known date that Lincoln came to Danville was on Monday, May 7, 1841. In a letter to a friend by the name of W.H. Davidson, Lincoln wrote (June 4, 1841), "... Baker and I were with Webb at Vermilion."

There is a record of his appearance in the local court on Tuesday, May 7, 1850, and from that time on, he attended the April and October sessions until 1859.

One of the most important events during this period from the standpoint of local interest was the formation of a law partnership with Ward Hill Lamon of this city, the man who was destined to become Lincoln's closest friend and bodyguard during the years in Washington.

A professional card appeared in the November 10, 1852, editions of the *Illinois Citizen* and the *Prairie State,* announcing the new law firm. The Barnum building referred to in the advertisement was on the present site of Bresee Tower.

By 1858, his political career was claiming most of Lincoln's attention. On September 21 of that year, he arrived in Danville on his campaign tour against Stephen A. Douglas for the United States Senate. He was to spend the night at the home of his friend and client, Dr. William E. Fithian (now the location of the Vermilion County Museum) at Gilbert and Lafayette streets.

A crowd of friends who heard Douglas speak that day September 21, 1858, (in a grove that is now Douglas Park) gathered under Lincoln's window and clamored for a speech.

He came out on the balcony and chatted humorously with the crowd, saying that he couldn't get his boots on to come down because his feet had swollen. The following day he delivered his formal reply to Douglas.

While in Danville, Abe "put up" at the McCormack House, which was located just west of the present site of the First National Bank drive-in complex. And he spent much of his leisure time visiting Dr. W.W.R. Woodbury and loafing in the latter's drug store (across W. Main St. to the east), telling the priceless anecdotes for which he became so well-known.

Lamon, a native Virginian, lived on W. North Street west of Gilbert, in a home no longer in existence. Although nominally a Democrat, he became one of Lincoln's staunchest political allies and played a leading role in the latter's nomination for president in 1860. He accompanied the president-elect to Washington as bodyguard.

Another great good friend of Lincoln in Danville was Oliver L. Davis, for 50 years a lawyer and judge. He was Lincoln's floor manager at the Wigwam convention hall in Chicago in 1860.

One final note about Lincoln in Danville: It was while attending court here that he decided to accept the invitation to address the Cooper Union in New York City. It was that speech, historians generally agree, that led him to the White House and his appointment with destiny.

His law clients in the 1850s saw a clean-shaven Lincoln, much as did photographer Amon Joslin, who took this picture in Danville in April, 1858. Lincoln did not grow a beard until after his election to the presidency in 1860. A young girl wrote him a letter, urging him to do so, saying that she thought it would make him look more "presidential."

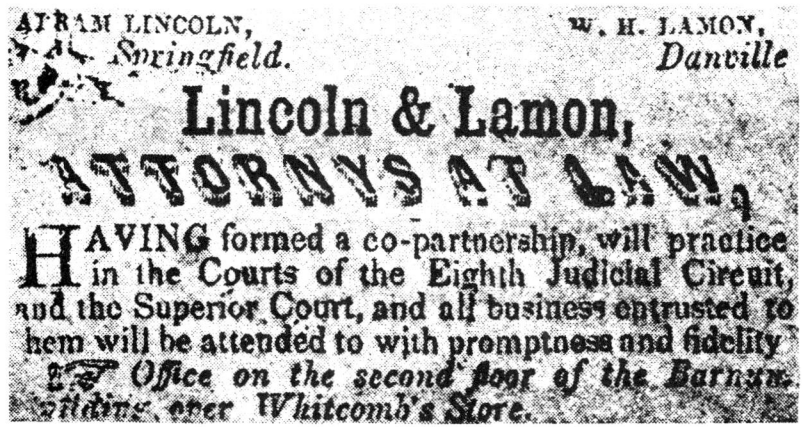

## DASHING OFFICER

Ward Hill Lamon, Lincoln's Danville law partner, had trimmed his heavy mustache to military style in this photograph made from a cracked glass negative. He had just raised a regiment at his own expense ($22,000) and been commissioned as colonel, a rank he would retain for the duration of the Civil War. But after seven months in the field, he was recalled to Washington.

It was on the second floor of the Barnum Building, wooden frame building above, that Lincoln and Lamon had their law offices in the 1850s. The location was 4 W. Main, later to be the site of the First National Bank. There is some question that this picture was taken then; legend has it that the building was moved to an E. Main Street location with the lower floor housing the War Museum Saloon. The structure later was destroyed by fire.

## CELEBRATED CONFINES

Judge Oliver Davis presided in circuit court in Danville in pre-Civil War days and was a friend and political ally of Abraham Lincoln. Davis was Lincoln's floor manager at the 1860 Republican national convention in Chicago. This was held in a large frame structure erected for the purpose by Gurdon Hubbard, a former Danville resident. The Wigwam had a capacity of something like 10,000 and was the scene of shrewd political maneuvering by Judge Davis, Judge David Davis (no relation) of Bloomington and Ward Hill Lamon, Lincoln's Danville law partner, to obtain Abe's nomination as president.

## FRIEND OF ABE

## DOCTOR'S HOME

This was the home of Dr. Theodore Lemon, a pioneer Danville physician, built in 1846 on Hazel Street, just south of Main. Although he spelled his name with an "e" instead of an "a", he was a cousin of Ward Hill Lamon and urged his young kinsman to move from Virginia to Danville. It was while rooming at Dr. Lemon's home that the transplanted young southerner became acquainted with Abraham Lincoln, the man who was destined to become his law partner and closest friend.

## WILLIAM FITHIAN

William Fithian was Danville's most prominent physician during most of the 19th century. He built the house that now is home to the Vermilion County Museum in 1855. There, Fithian played host to several famous political figures. One was his great friend, Abraham Lincoln.

Fithian, who was the first white child born in Cincinnati, learned printing there as a boy. He began to study medicine at 17 with money he had saved and came to Illinois from Indiana, settling in Danville in 1830.

Eventually, Fithian's practice extended as far west as Bloomington, south to Paris, north to Kankakee, and east far into Indiana. He put his savings into real estate, later donating land to the railroad where a town was to be built. They named the town Fithian.

Fithian and Lincoln were sworn into the Illinois House of Representatives together in 1834, after winning election on the same day.

Lincoln stopped by the Fithian home whenever he was in Danville, occasionally staying overnight. Fithian worked for the Lincoln organization in 1858 and 1860. His reward was appointment as provost marshal for the Seventh Illinois District.

Fithian continued to practice into his 80's. The doctor, born the year George Washington died, himself died in 1890, the year Dwight Eisenhower was born.

## LINCOLN SLEPT HERE

This was the home of Dr. William E. Fithian, pioneer Danville physician, friend and client of Abraham Lincoln. From the second floor balcony, visible through branches of tree, Lincoln addressed well-wishers while house-guest of Fithian. The occasion was a visit to Danville during the 1858 campaign for the U.S. Senate against Stephen A. Douglas. The house was built in 1855 and some remodeling was done in the 1890s, notably expansion of a front porch. Now the home of the Vermilion County Museum, it is listed on the register of National Historic Places.

## HOSPITALITY HOUSE

This was the home of Reason Hooton, prominent Danville resident of pre-Civil War days. He was fond of entertaining the lawyers who rode the old Eighth Illinois Judicial Circuit, providing wine of his own creation. Lincoln, a frequent guest, was known for his moderation in drinking but is supposed to have remarked to his fellow lawyers on one occasion: "Fellers, I'm getting drunk!" The house, in southeastern Danville, was torn down several years ago and the site is now occupied by the International Nursing Home.

## FAMOUS NAMESAKE

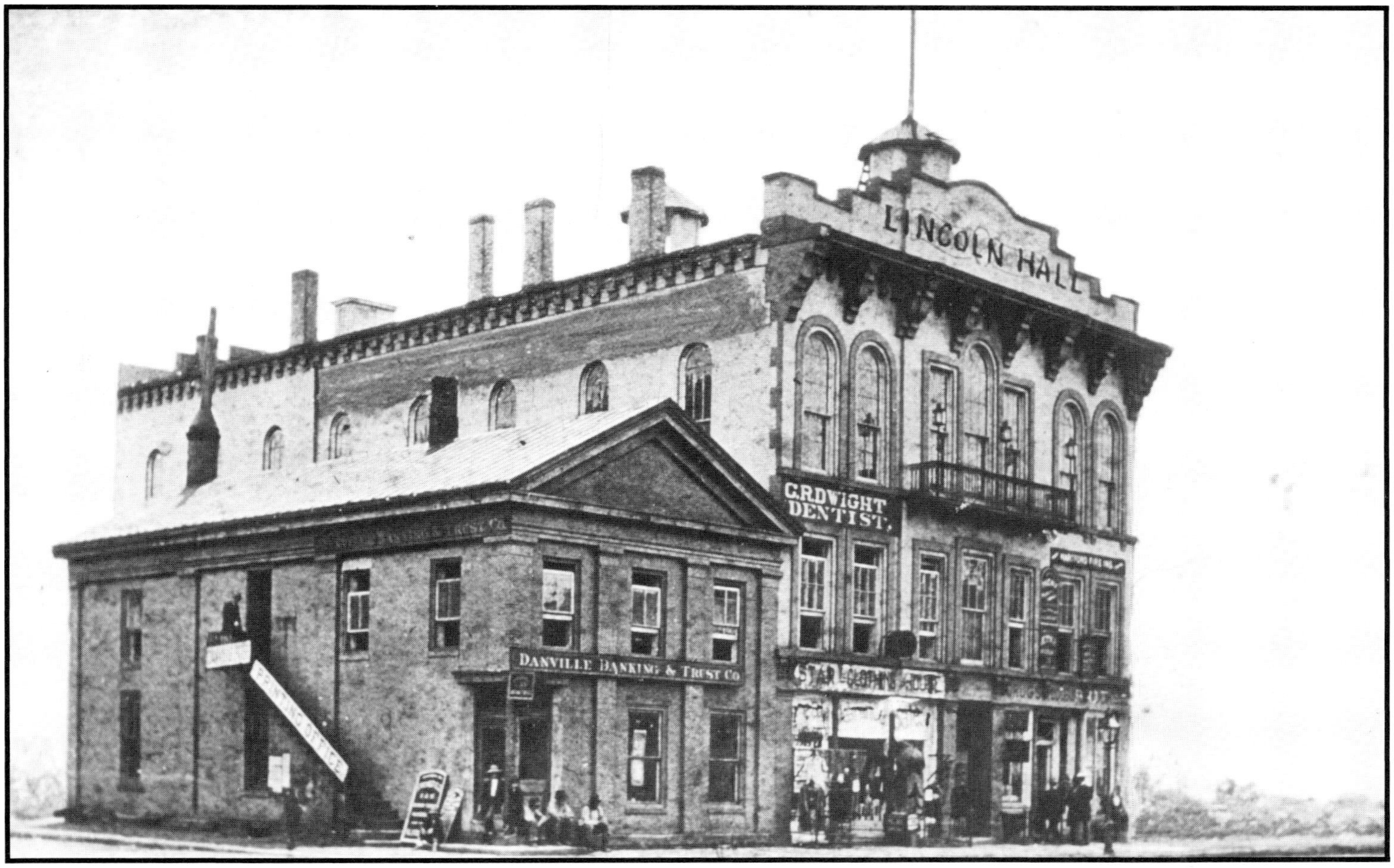

Lincoln Hall, built by Dr. W.W.R. Woodbury in 1859 on W. Main Street, was the only building to bear Abraham Lincoln's name during his lifetime. Dr. Woodbury's drugstore occupied the first-floor storeroom at right. The smaller building at left housed Danville Banking & Trust Company, which began operations in 1880 and merged with the Second National Bank in 1920. The site is now occupied by Palmer-American National Bank. Lincoln was a frequent visitor to Woodbury Drug Company's original store in an earlier building on the same site.

## GRACIOUS RESIDENCE

The Gustavus Pearson home, as it appears today, was a showplace from the mid-Nineteenth Century on. Known as "Glen Springs Farm," it was the residence of a man who made a fortune in California, as a merchant in the Gold Rush days. Springs provided water for the house and an adjoining barn. At one time, a dam south of the dwelling impounded overflow from the springs, creating a small lake. While in California, Pearson is credited with discovering Yosemite Valley, now a national park. His daughter, Frances Pearson Meeks, became an outstanding educator and was the wife of James A. Meeks, congressman from Danville in the 1930s.

## STURDY SURVIVOR

The present home of Jewell Whyte Post 728, Veterans of Foreign Wars, this old brick building has seen many occupants since its construction in 1850. Built by the Methodists, it was known as the Red Seminary and the main entrance was on W. Main Street (today, the porch and principal entrance face Pine Street). At various times, the building has housed the seminary, Eastern Illinois College, a public school and a private home. Between 1868 and 1884, the building was used for a time as part of the city school system. In 1884, Illinois Wesleyan University began operating the school as a preparatory institution but withdrew in 1887 upon learning that its charter allowed operation in Bloomington only.

The "White," or more properly the Union Seminary, was built by the Presbyterians on the northeast corner of Vermilion and Seminary Streets in 1851. It continued until 1862, when the common school system was adopted for the city. The building burned around 1871. No known photograph of it exists.

## HANDSOME EDIFICE

This 1875 photograph shows the handsome North Street Methodist Church, situated on the southeast corner of North and Vermilion Streets. It was built in 1857 at a cost of $13,500 and served the congregation until 1889. The first union service in commemoration of Decoration (later Memorial) Day in 1869 was held here. For some reason lost in the mist of history, Danville did not observe formally the first holiday in 1868.

## HISTORIC HOME

This little white cottage first located at 302 W. North Street was the home of Ward Hill Lamon's cousin, Joseph Lamon, and his wife, Melissa, daughter of Dan Beckwith. Joseph was instrumental in persuading his cousin to come to Danville from Virginia; no doubt Hill Lamon and Abraham Lincoln often called on the Joseph Lamons here. The cottage was saved from the wrecker's hammer, was moved to a permanent site in Lincoln Park and restored to its 1850 condition by public subscription.

## FIRST TRAIN

This was the scene in October, 1856, as the *Pioneer,* the first train to come into Danville, chugged across the old wooden bridge over the Vermilion River, south of South Street. The railroad was the Northern Cross, predecessor of the Great Western, Wabash, Norfolk & Western and Norfolk & Southern railroads. Sketch was made by Mariah Williams, 29-year-old daughter of Amos Williams, who was one of the prime movers in the effort to bring the railroad to Danville.

## ANCIENT TAVERN

The Treat Tavern was host to travelers in Denmark, an early-day suburb of Danville, for many years. Denmark's demise was due to its lurid reputation for gambling, horse racing and drunken brawls. This picture of the tavern was taken in 1916; building was razed prior to area's flooding by the waters of Lake Vermilion in 1925.

## HOME OF A HERO

The Oscar F. Harmon home at 522 E. Main Street actually was a farm house, inasmuch as the property comprised 30 tillable acres, extending east and south from the corner of Main and Elizabeth Streets, then on the outskirts of town. Remodeled extensively since the 1850s, it has been used as a funeral home and as a halfway house for the rehabilitation of alcohol and substance abuse victims.

Oscar F. Harmon, according to Vermilion County historian Hiram Beckwith, "was much above the average height, being six feet, three inches, and well-proportioned mentally, morally and physically. No better man of the regiment could be found to be their commander." He was referring to Harmon's appointment as colonel of the Civil War 125th Illinois Volunteer Infantry Regiment. It was organized in Danville and consisted of seven companies from Vermilion County and three from Champaign.

Harmon, a native of Monroe County, New York, came to Danville in 1853 at age 26 and was the law partner of Judge Oliver L. Davis. In 1857, he served as state representative from Vermilion County.

The 125th, with Harmon as its commander, participated in the battles of Perryville, Chickamauga, Mission Ridge and the Atlanta campaign. During the latter, while leading a charge up Kenesaw Mountain in Georgia, Col. Harmon was shot and killed on June 27, 1864. He was 37.

He was married in 1854 to a widow, Mrs. E.C. Hill, whose maiden name was McDonald. Harmon Avenue was named in his honor.

# HOME, SWEET HOME

Gustavus C. Pearson and family pose in this photo made from a tintype about 1875. His conservative attire belies Pearson's adventurous nature. He made serveral trips around Cape Horn to the Pacific coast to engage in commercial trade in California. He was a member of the first party of white men to cross Death Valley on foot and live to tell the tale. Although he became wealthy from his business ventures in the West, he kept Danville as his home. This picture shows Glen Springs, the home he had built many years before, on Elizabeth Street. It is still standing.

## FAMILY PRIDE

All dressed up in their Sunday best, the Larry Jones family poses for a group picture in one of Danville's photo galleries. In his youth, Jones had the distinction of being the first stagecoach driver in Vermilion County. As such, he no doubt often announced the arrival of the mail by blowing on a conch horn from atop the South Danville hill that led down to the ferry crossing of the Vermilion River. Others in photo are not identified but it is presumed that the children are the Joneses grandchildren.

BRINGING CHANGE

---
## CHAPTER II
---
# WAR
# AND
# PEACE
---
### 1861 - 1890
---

By 1860, Danville long since had abandoned Dan Beckwith's dream of being a river town. But its location on trails naturally used by pioneers encouraged the development of roads and consequent growth as a trading center. In the year before the Civil War began, the city's population was 1,632.

Yet, it was the advent of railroad transportation that would boost Danville from a figurative "wide place in the road" to a middle-sized city. The Great Western, previously known as the Northern Cross, had reached the city from the west in 1856, thus linking Danville with Quincy on the Mississippi River. Connection with the east slowed until after the conclusion of the Civil War.

Vermilion County had come into being as a governmental entity in January, 1826, and Danville, as county seat, some 15 months later. But in the early years, the county as such, with the establishment of many other communities, had grown much more rapidly than the city. In 1860, Vermilion's population was 19,779; Danville's share of this figure was only 8¼ per cent. This trend would begin to reverse itself soon to such a remarkable degree that in 1987, some 45 per cent of the people in Vermilion County would reside within Danville's corporate limits.

Although weekly newspapers were published in Danville as early as 1832, the first daily publications of any size and influence did not appear until after the Civil War.

The first newspaper was the *Weekly Inquirer*, a Democratic organ, put out by a man named Williams (no relation to Amos Williams) and an R.H. Bryant.

"The first pioneer newspapers filled a very definite need in the Danville area," says Richard Lee Hare in *100 Years of Newspapers in Danville, Illinois*, published in 1966, "and along with the Bible provided the community with the major portion of its literature."

The *Patriot* was founded in 1843, presumably as a successor to the *Inquirer*. "The Danville of 1846 is best pictured through advertisements (in the *Patriot*)," says Hare. "Wool carding appeared to be the greatest industry, the early settlers taking their wool to these mills for carding, after which the pioneer spinning wheels were used for turning it into cloth for the crude clothing of the day."

Then followed the *Illinois Citizen* in 1849, the *Prairie State* in 1856, the *Independent* in 1857, the *Danville Republican* in 1859 and the *Vermilion County Press* in 1860.

The *Danville Commercial*, which survived to become a daily, was founded in 1866, the *Danville News* in 1873, the *Danville Press* in 1887 and the *Danville Democrat* 10 years later. These four newspapers ultimately consolidated and exist in 1987 as the *Commercial-News*.

Log cabins as dwellings and places of business had disappeared almost completely from the scene in Danville by 1860. Frame buildings, with material from the city's numerous sawmills, had taken their place. But this "progress" did not alleviate the ever-present danger of fire.

Plans for a fire department got underway in 1858 and by 1859, the first primitive pieces of equipment were bought and a fire station erected on the present-day site of the Palmer-American National Bank. In 1861, the department got its first hand pumps.

Six years later the department reorganized and became Lincoln Fire Company No. 1. Another reorganization occurred in 1872 and a steam fire engine (for pumping water) was purchased.

A third reorganization in 1879 established the monthly salary of the chief at $55. Pay for the volunteer firemen ranged from $13 monthly to $13 per quarter.

Early Danville was policed by constables and, because it was the county seat, by sheriff's deputies if reinforcements were needed. But the need for an organized, larger law enforcement body is pointed out in this article from the September 9, 1869, *Danville Commercial:* "We are requested to call the attention of the city authorities to the almost nightly disturbances that take place on Vermilion Street after the saloons have closed. We would suggest the propriety of having more police, as it is impossible for one or two men to keep watch over all the city."

Dr. Asa Palmer, a native of New York, was this city's first phycian, arriving here in 1825. Dr. William Fithian followed in 1830.

Dr. W.W.R. Woodbury also was one of the first druggists in Danville. Dr. George Wheeler Jones, who came to the city immediately after the Civil War, also set up a drugstore with his brother.

In 1868, a group of doctors met at Lincoln Hall to form a medical association "for the advancement of the profession toward the distant goal of perfection," as the *Danville Commercial* put it. But the Vermilion County Medical Society, as we know it today, wasn't founded until November 12, 1879.

Dentists were not as quick to choose Danville for their practice; as late as 1884, there were only five practitioners in the county.

Four sisters of St. Francis of the Sacred Heart came to Danville in 1882 to care for the sick, working in a 14-room converted hotel called the Indiana House, which stood on the corner of Green (now Sager) and Elizabeth Streets. This was the first St. Elizabeth Hospital. In 1888, work was started on a three-story, 48-room brick building, which was dedicated in 1889. Eighty patient beds were provided.

In 1883, the Danville Water Company began exercising the franchise it had obtained the year before from the Danville City Council. Its first--and only--business was supplying ample water from the North Fork River for fire protection. For several years, it was occupied with laying mains and installing fire hydrants. With every home and business establishment providing its own drinking water from wells, there simply was no market for many years.

Telegraph service came to Danville in 1852 and Western Union took over the first office in 1867. The first telephone in the city was installed on September 20, 1879, in the Danville *Daily News* office. And a year-and-a-half after the first electric light plant was opened in the United States, Danville had lights. The Merchants' Electric Light and Power Company, organized in 1883, went into operation early in 1884.

Danville's economy grew in the 1860-1890 period with the location of new businesses. The Vermilion County Bank was opened by William P. and Joseph G. Cannon in 1873 at 15 E. Main Street. It became the Second National Bank. And the First National Bank, which was opened in 1857, built a handsome two-story brick building on the public square in 1870. Under the 1863 National Banking Act, the First National (as it became known) was the third bank in Illinois to be chartered.

Schools were built, including Washington in 1871 and Danville High in 1889, and on July 21, 1882, the Danville Public Library Board first met at the Arlington Hotel. And the following February 22, the McDonald room on the second floor of the building west of the First National on Main Street was rented for $72 per year. The Rev. James Coe, rector of Holy Trinity Church, was hired as librarian. In 1885, new quarters were rented and the library moved to a second-floor location about where the Sears, Roebuck store is today.

---

HANDSOME HOTEL

This elegant hotel was opened July 4, 1876, and was christened the Centennial. When this photograph was taken in 1880, the hostelry had been renamed the Arlington. This view is toward the west and north, probably from an upper story of Lincoln Hall, across W. Main Street to the south and east. The small white frame building with galleried porch adjacent to the three-story hotel building is the McCormack House, Danville's first hotel, where Abraham Lincoln was a frequent guest. The building in background, top left, is the old Red Seminary, only survivor of structures shown. In modern times, the Arlington site was occupied by the Grier-Lincoln Hotel, and now contains the drive-in facilities of the First National Bank.

# DANVILLE AND THE CIVIL WAR

To quote from Jack M. Williams' *History of Vermilion County:* "Vermilion County made a remarkable showing in the Civil War, not only in the number of enlistments but in the gallantry of its troops in the field . . . the county sent 2,596 soldiers into the various military organizations, or 12½ percent of its entire population."

The following military units had men from Danville in their ranks: Fourth Illinois Cavalry, 12th Illinois Infantry, 25th Illinois Infantry, 35th Illinois Infantry, 37th Illinois Infantry, 71st Illinois Infantry, 73rd Illinois Infantry, 51st Illinois Infantry, 125th Illinois Infantry, 135th Illinois Infantry, 149th Illinois Infantry, 150th Illinois Infantry, the 28th (Consolidated) Illinois Infantry.

In addition to the regiments named above, Vermilion County men (with some undoubtedly from Danville) were found in at least half of the other regiments of the state. Thirty-six men went from the county to Col. Richard Oglesby's Eighth Illinois Infantry.

Danville soldiers were involved in many famous battles, sieges and skirmishes from early in the war to the very last day. The 12th, for example, participated in the capture of strategic Fort Donelson, suffered heavy losses in the Battle of Shiloh, took part in the siege and capture of Corinth, Mississippi, saw action in the siege and capture of Atlanta and was with Sherman on his March to the Sea.

Several Danville men attained high rank and achieved great distinction. Among these were Col. John C. Black, later a brigadier general; Col. Othniel Gilbert; Col. W.P. Chandler; Col. Oscar Harmon, who fell at Kenesaw Mountain, and Capt. William Black. The 37th, commanded by Col. Black, assaulted and captured Fort Blakely, guarding Mobile, Alabama, in the last battle of the war on April 9, 1865.

## DASHING CAPTAIN

Capt. John Moran of Danville was a company commander in the 37th Illinois Volunteer Infantry Regiment which saw nearly five years' service in the Civil War, including the last battle, the capture of Fort Blakely and the city of Mobile, Alabama.

Col. W.P. Chandler of Danville, commanding officer of the 35th Illinois Volunteer Infantry Regiment, distinguished himself at the Battle of Mission Ridge in Tennessee, November 23-25, 1863. According to historian Jack M. Williams: ". . . the regiment was placed in a most dangerous and important position, being in the front line, and displayed great valor and coolness in being led to within 20 steps of the rebel works on the crest of the hill. In the assault, all of the color guard were shot down and Col. Chandler carried the flag into the enemy's works, followed by his men."

## HE CARRIED THE FLAG

## OFFICERS OF THE 37TH

One of the outstanding infantry regiments from Illinois, indeed, of the entire Union, in the Civil War was the 37th. Three of its officers from the Danville area were, left to right, Lt. Col. E.B. Payne, Capt. George R. Bell and Capt. Joe Wolford. The regiment marched four times from the Great Lakes to the Gulf of Mexico and journeyed by water transportation nearly 10,000 miles. It took part in 13 battles and skirmishes and two great sieges.

## A HERO'S DEATH

This artist's sketch shows how Col. Oscar F. Harmon of Danville, commanding officer of the 125th Illinois Volunteer Infantry Regiment, lost his life in the Battle of Kenesaw Mountain on June 27, 1864. He was shot by a Confederate sharpshooter while leading his men up the steep heights of the mountain, one of the obstacles to the Union Army's advance on Atlanta. One-half of the regiment's 900 men (70 percent were from Danville and Vermilion County) were killed or wounded in the battle.

CIVIL WAR HERO...

... AND A HERO'S BROTHER

John Charles Black, stepson of pioneer physician, William Fithian, was Danville's No. 1 hero of the Civil War. He dropped out of Wabash College in Crawfordsville, Indiana, helped organize the 37th Illinois Volunteer Infantry Regiment and rose through the officer ranks to colonel and commanding officer. He was the first U.S. soldier to be awarded the Congressional Medal of Honor. He led the successful assault on Fort Blakely, guarding Mobile, Alabama, in the final battle of the war and was promoted to brevet brigadier general. He was 26 years old at the time.

William P. Black, John C. Black's brother, graduated from Wabash College in the class of 1864 but immediately enlisted in his brother's regiment, the 37th Illinois Volunteer Infantry. He quickly rose to a captaincy and was a company commander at the Battle of Pea Ridge in Arkansas. It was there that he, like his brother, won the Congressional Medal of Honor. It is the only instance in U.S. military history where brothers have been awarded the nation's highest decoration for valor.

## MUCH TRAVELED VETERAN

William M. Bandy of Danville had the distinction of serving as adjutant of both the 37th and 125th Illinois Volunteer Infantry Regiments in the Civil War. While with the 37th, he participated in the victorious siege of Vicksburg and his name is inscribed on the Illinois memorial at the battle scene. Later, he was with the 125th during the march on Atlanta that culminated in the capture of that city.

## POPULAR GENERAL

Maj. Gen. John A. Logan of Illinois was popular in Danville and among local Civil War troops. He was the uncle of Sally Logan, the second Mrs. Ward Hill Lamon (the first wife of Danville's former Lincoln law partner died). After the war, Mill Street in this city was renamed in honor of Gen. Logan, who also is credited with founding the postwar observance of Decoration Day, later Memorial Day.

## MAKING MUSICAL HISTORY

W.F. Heath, bandmaster of the 146th Regimental Band, 146th Illinois Volunteer Infantry Regiment of the Civil War, second from left, led the funeral march of Abraham Lincoln in Springfield in 1865. His Danville connection? The special music score he composed for the occasion is supposed to have remained unclaimed in a safe deposit box in a Danville bank for many years. And Heath wound up as the bandmaster at the old Soldiers Home in Danville after the turn of the century.

# COAL MINING

The presence of coal in Vermilion County was discovered by the early settlers. Strip bank mining was started in the early 1850s.

Dudley Lacock, who owned considerable land west of Danville, is credited with mining the first commercial coal. But there was such little demand for it that he gave up and moved to Livingston County in 1854.

William Kirkland opened drift mines east of the Wabash Railroad (now the Norfolk & Southern) bridge across the Vermilion River in the 1850s. The first extensive mining was done by Chandler & Donlan in 1860. They were followed by Peter Leonard.

Hungry Hollow was the first area of intensive mining. Henry Cramer, who had settled there with his family in 1862, opened a strip bank three years later.

But the real beginning of the industry was in 1866 when William Kirkland, Hugh Blakeney, a Mrs. Graves and a Mr. Lafferty opened strip mines in the Grape Creek area.

The first underground mining was begun by A.C. Daniel, who sank a shaft in 1870 for the Ellsworth Coal Company. He sank another for the same firm two years later.

West Vermilion Heights also became a coal center in 1870, when John C. Short, one of the founders of the *Danville Commercial*, opened the Moss Bank mine.

In 1883, the first annual coal report of the state of Illinois showed coal mine employment in Vermilion County as 1,061.

The first strip mining by mechanical means took place in 1885. River dredges were used to remove 35 feet of overburden from a 6-foot vein of coal. But numerous costly problems arose and the dredges were abandoned in 1890.

The greatest number of shipping mines in the county was reached in 1890, when 64 were in production.

---

MINE MOGUL

A.C. Daniel came to Danville in 1857 as an ambitious 22-year-old with the clothes on his back and $2.50. The young New Yorker immediately went to work in the mines, doing odd jobs for the Kirkland Brothers mining operation. Before 25 years had passed, Daniel would control almost all coal mines near Danville. Some called him "the father of underground mining."

Daniel's meteoric rags-to-riches climb began with a partnership with Roswell Smith of Lafayette, Indiana, who later was to found Century Magazine. In the late 1860s, Daniel helped organize the Ellsworth Coal Company. By 1879, when Ellsworth bought out the Carbon Coal Company, Daniel had become general manager and principal stockholder of the company. All these mines were then combined into the Consolidated Coal Company, which Daniel helped to organize.

Not only did Daniel advance mining in the area, he also was instrumental in the growth of South Danville. Most of the people living there worked for Daniel's mines south and west of the city, including the present site of Ellsworth Park.

The lack of a good education had hurt him, he realized, and he consistently recognized the value of education. He served on the Danville board of education, hoping his workers' children would have a better start. He also helped organize the mule-powered Danville streetcar system in 1884, and developed property in downtown Danville.

Daniel died in Danville in 1907 a rich man. But he never forgot his humble beginnings.

These miners are resting in a room in a deep coal mine in the Danville Field in 1925--but the scene could just as easily have been photographed in 1890. The field had a "good-news-bad-news" reputation: The roof in the tunnels was unstable but the mines were free of gas.

IRISH 'LUCK'

Among the millions of Irish immigrants to this country in the 1850's was a short, stocky 20-year-old named Mike Kelly. When thousands went west to go into farming, Kelly went, too. But Kelly was destined to never lift the plow.

The young Irishman worked on the engine of a wood-burning train to earn his passage from Pennsylvania to Illinois in 1859. He told the train's engineer of his ambition to get cheap land. But the engineer told Kelly it was coal he should look for, and he knew just where to look.

So Kelly came to Danville and took up work in a mine near Hungry Hollow, west of town. A few years later, Kelly bought the mine from its discouraged owner for $160.

Kelly soon found a new vein in the old mine, and secured a contract to supply the Chicago and Eastern Illinois Railroad. He found another vein 90 feet down. From there, Kelly's business snowballed. He opened more mines in 1888 and bought out the Himrod Mines in 1903.

His 8,000 acres and six mines made him the biggest single coal mine operator in the United States. When he sold his mines in 1905, the price was $3 million.

SISTERS COURAGEOUS

Four Franciscan nuns came to Danville in 1882 to care for the sick. They started a hospital in a converted hotel but seven years later dedicated a new, three-story, 48-room, 80-bed hospital.

IS IT DANVILLE OR PARIS?

The Aetna House on the corner of North and Vermilion Streets in 1880 had a distinctly Parisian air, enhanced by the gas lamp on the corner, the trees in leaf and the row of chimneys adorning the roof. Legend has it that the hotel was opened with a grand ball on the night President Abraham Lincoln was assassinated--April 14, 1865.

# EARLY RAILROADS

In 1856, the *Pioneer* pulled a Great Western train across the Vermilion River bridge, highest span in Illinois, into Danville.

The Great Western Railroad, originally the Northern Cross, was supposed to link Quincy, Illinois, with the Toledo and Wabash Railroad, approaching from the east. But there was disagreement and the latter road withdrew to State Line, Indiana, forcing the Great Western to go there. For eight years, both roads had shops and fuel depots in that town. The two roads consolidated in 1865 and the united line took the name Wabash.

According to *History Under Our Feet* (Stapp and Bowman); "The terminal was moved to Danville shortly afterwards for two reasons: Danville was gaining prominence as a coal-producing center and the water of the Vermilion River and Stony Creek was softer and less lime producing." (Lime corroded the interior of locomotive boilers.--Editor) The road operated a roundhouse between Main and South Streets until 1882, when the entire operation was moved to Tilton to get closer to the sources of coal.

The big need was for a connection to Chicago. In 1865, a group of investors wanted to build a line connecting Vincennes, Indiana and Chicago by way of Paris and Danville, but ran into financial difficulty. Danville Township voted to give $72,000 if the route was guaranteed to pass through the city. The offer was accepted and operation began in 1871. Later another financial incentive was offered if the road would establish repair shops here. The original shops were built east of the Wabash Railroad, just south of E. Fairchild Street; they were relocated in Oaklawn in 1904.

Another road coming from the west where it served Bloomington, Pekin and Urbana joined one coming from Indianapolis by way of Crawfordsville in 1884. Danville Township helped this venture by investing $100,000 in stock. This became the Big Four and finally Peoria & Eastern.

A line north and south through the city was built in 1889.

Where these three roads intersected at a point between Collett Street and what became known as Junction Avenue, there developed a kind of union station complex titled Danville Junction. It would become a colorful chapter in the city's railroading history.

PRIDE OF THE SEVENTIES

This was one of the first locomotives to pull trains over the C&EI Railroad tracks into Danville back in 1873. That the men who operated and maintained this shiny engine were very proud of it is evident in their posture.

Hi Gene allen
Glad to be here for your "surprise" - Lots of good memories Love Lela

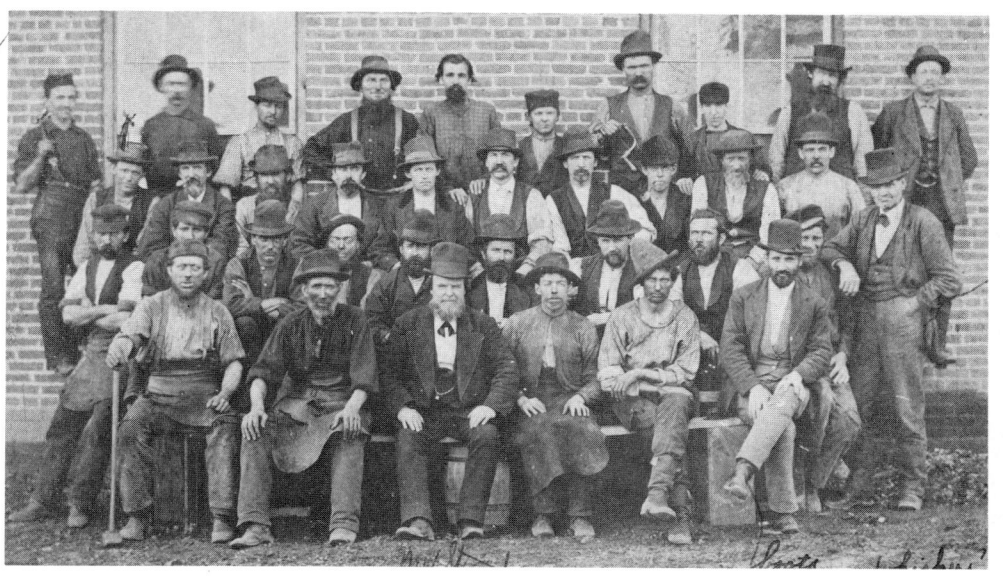

ROUGH AND READY CREW

These employees of the Stuart-Holmes Shop near the C&EI Railroad tracks at Junction Avenue and Williams Street obviously were not hired for their personal appearance but no doubt were competent in their blacksmithing and foundry duties. The men seated third from left in the front row, wearing the high hat, white shirt and tie and sporting a gold watch chain is identified as Mr. Stuart, apparently the senior partner of the firm. Photograph was taken in 1876.

Locomotive No. 73 of the Chicago & Eastern Illinois Railroad, the C&EI, appears to be brand-spanking new as the date on the photograph would seem to attest--and the poses of the road crew indicate. The scene probably was outside the engine houses of the first C&EI shops in Danville, located just off E. Fairchild Street, east of Danville High School and the Wabash Railroad tracks. These shops were vacated shortly after the turn of the century in favor of the new and much larger Oaklawn shops.

PROUD RAILROADERS

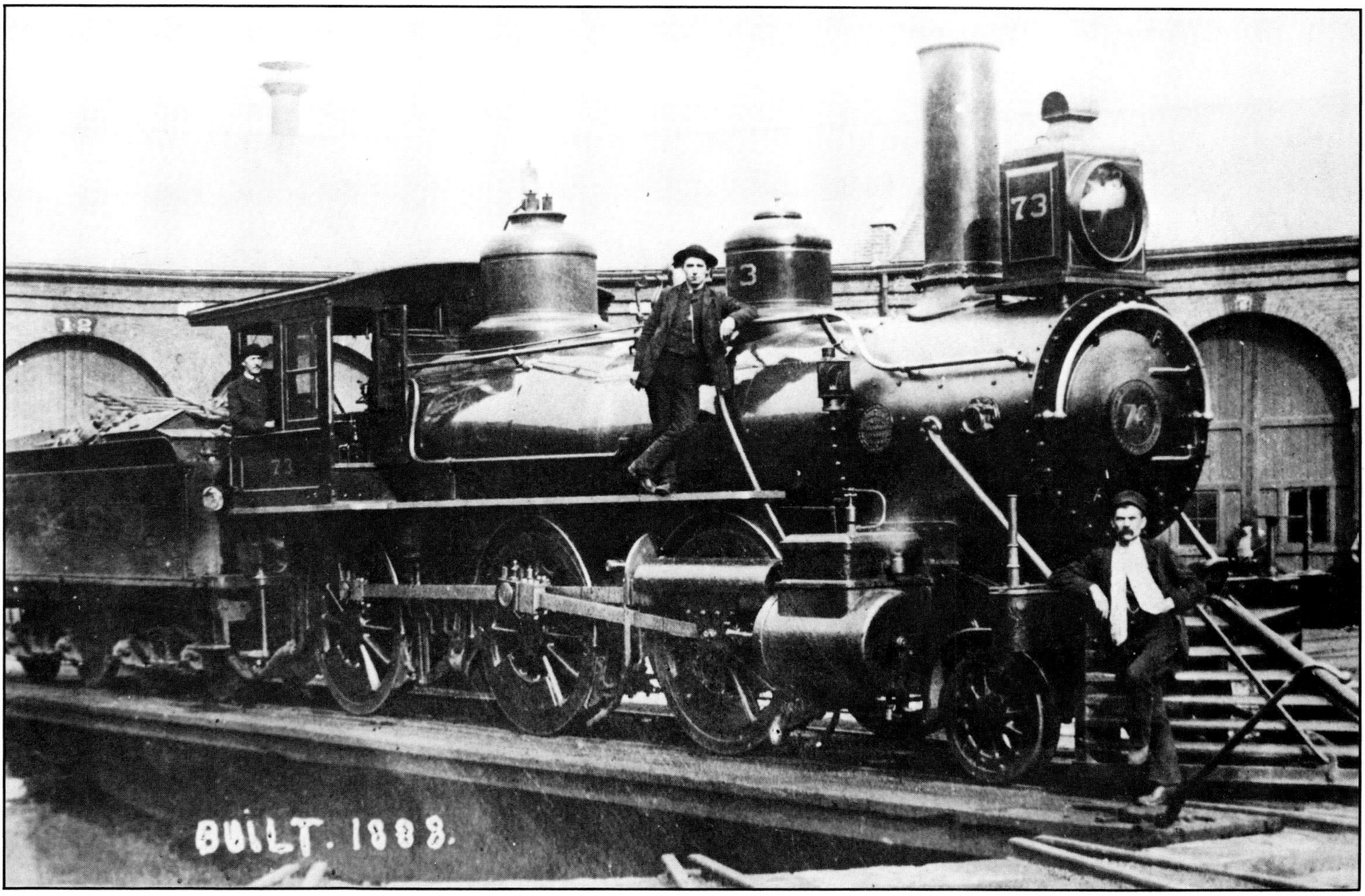

MAYOR JASPER WINSLOW

Danville's first mayor was probably its most accomplished and academic chief executive. Jasper C. Winslow, a Vermont native, was successful at each of the many occupations he tried.

Winslow left home at 14 to teach music and then to manufacture musical instruments. After several years, he joined the Saratoga and Schenectady Railroad in New York, leaving to become master mechanic of the New York and New Haven Road. He came to the Midwest as assistant master mechanic of the Great Western Railroad, later to become the Wabash. But he gave up railroading in 1859, turning down a promotion to master mechanic.

Coming to Danville in 1860, Winslow concentrated on two other interests--dentistry and geology. He opened a dentist's office in the old Vermilion Opera House building (on the northeast corner of Vermilion and North Streets) and pursued geological studies throughout the county with Professor William Gurley. Winslow became known as an authority in geology, and was quoted in Europe as well as in the United States.

Danville acted to incorporate as a city when rules were set down by the state in 1867. In May, 1868, Dr. Winslow was elected the city's first mayor under its new charter. The city purchased its first fire engine while Winslow was mayor.

After his retirement from office, Winslow helped found the Vermilion County Historical Society in 1877, and served as manager and curator. He also was a founder of the Episcopalian Church of the Holy Trinity.

Winslow died in 1886.

## DISTINCTIVE ARCHITECTURE

The Italianate style of architecture was much favored when the Vermilion County Jail was built in 1874. For many years--in fact, until the mid-20th century--the jail also served as the residence of the sheriff. An annex was built onto the north side of the building in the early 1920s. Until the state of Illinois accepted the responsibility in the late 1920s, many executions by hanging were carried out in the jail. It served nearly a century until replaced by the contemporary Public Safety Building.

## FROM THE OLD MILL STREAM

This top millstone saw plenty of service when it was part of the old Gilbert Mill, which was located at the confluence of the North Fork and Salt Fork rivers in the southwest corner of what is today Ellsworth Park. The stone now rests on the lawn of the Vermilion County Museum.

## CHOICE VINDICATED

One of the reasons Danville was chosen as county seat was because the site was 90 feet above encompassing river banks, hence safe from floods. This picture of the Vermilion River at flood stage, some time between 1885 and 1890, demonstrates how correct that reasoning was. This view is from the north bank, looking southwest toward the old Red Bridge, linking Danville and South Danville.

## ELEGANT EDIFICE

This was the First Methodist Episcopal Church (later renamed St. James) at the corner of N. Vermilion and E. Williams Streets. It was built in 1889 to replace the North Street Methodist Church on the corner of North and Vermilion Streets. The larger church served congregations for 40 years, being succeeded by the present St. James United Methodist Church, cater-cornered across the intersection. The photograph at left was taken about 1910. Note streetcar tracks and overhead wires; tracks turning the corner served Danville Junction.

## HEALING THE RIFT

The Presbyterian church in the United States was divided in some bitterness because of the Civil War. Members in Danville, staunch defenders of the Union, nevertheless viewed the dedication of their new edifice in 1865 (on the site of the contemporary church) as a symbol of renewed unity among Presbyterians everywhere in the nation.

## HUMBLE BEGINNING

The Second Baptist Church, serving many black residents of Danville, had its start here in 1889. The frame structure, on the north side of Kimber Street between Harmon Avenue and Chandler Street, later was brick-veneered. The congregation ultimately moved to 935 Oak Street, where it occupies a handsome edifice. Other denominations occupied the building after the Baptists left, including one known in the neighborhood as "the holy rollers." The first black religious organization in the city was Allen Chapel Methodist Episcopal, formed in 1872. Its first church was erected in 1877. Today's edifice is situated on the corner of N. Jackson and W. Williams Streets.

St. Augustine Catholic Church was built in 1874 on the northeast corner of N. Washington Avenue and E. Harrison Street, and served black communicants of the faith. As parishioners transferred to other Catholic churches, membership dwindled and the church closed. For a while, the building was used for commerical purposes but was torn down many years ago.

## CHURCH OF THE PAST

## FAMILIAR LANDMARK

Danville Episcopalians have worshiped in this same building, the Church of the Holy Trinity at 308 N. Vermilion Street, for more then 118 years. A frame structure originally, it was dedicated in 1869, and brick-veneered 50 years later in 1919. This photograph was taken in 1900 to show the church's new tower and front window. The man in the picture is Dr. F.W. Taylor.

## MUCH FOR THE MONEY

It cost $3,035 to build the German United Brethren Church at E. North and Hayes streets in 1871. Note the muddy condition of the unpaved roadway (North Street). The site is now occupied by buildings of the Lauhoff Grain Company complex.

## REVERENTLY REMEMBERED

This comparatively modern photograph is of St. Patrick's Catholic Church, built in 1880 at the corner of E. Main and Park Streets. It was the spiritual home of Danville's east side Catholics for a century until its demolition in 1980. St. Joseph's Catholic Church, also established in the latter half of the 19th century and located south and east of St. Patrick's, served parishioners of German ancestry but closed in the 1970s. The congregation joined that of St. Patrick's under the name of Holy Family Church. Worship is conducted in a new edifice of modernistic design built in the 1980s and located on the original site.

## UNUSUAL DESIGN

The turrets flanking the front of the First Church of Christ gave it an unusual appearance. The building, measuring 34 by 55 feet in size, was built in 1874 at a cost of $3,500. Later, the congregation built a large brick church on the corner of Oak and Seminary. Ultimately, they merged with the Third Church to form Central Christian Church, whose modern edifice is situated just north of English Street on the east side of Vermilion Street. The building in the photograph was converted into an apartment building which was torn down in 1986. The site is now a parking lot for the Assembly of God Church on Walnut Street.

## IMPOSING EDIFICE

The First Baptist Church was an imposing edifice when it was built in 1874 on the corner of Madison and Walnut Streets, facing west. It served the congregation well for 40 years, before a large brick building was erected two blocks north, on the corner of Walnut and W. Williams Streets. The church's current home, together with a parochial school, is located on the east side of N. Vermilion Street in the 1200 block.

## HARDLY A SISSY

Don't left the Gay Nineties' Beau Brummell attire fool you! Loren Shutts was at least a six-footer and an athlete as well—which he needed to be to ride the high-wheel bicycle. In some models, the front wheel was 64 inches high and the rear 12. You needed strength, agility and a fine sense of balance to master these machines. This picture was taken in 1890.

This was Danville's first cycling club—in 1889. These dashing athletes are, left to right: Front row—Charles Abdill, George Wright, Carroll Williams, George Gordon, Gardie Woodbury; middle row—Dick Cannon, Oscar Greenebaum, Clarence Brittingham; top row—Charles Daniels, Ed Black, Charles M. Woodbury, Will Connelly, George Learnard. Daniels and Learnard are holding the latest models of the new so-called "safety" bicycles. Woodbury's bike was the old model with a five-foot high front wheel.

## DASHING CYCLISTS

FOREVER FOOD

August Faulstich owned and operated this popular east side grocery on the corner of Main and Buchanan Streets for many years. It may be August himself standing in front of the store while his delivery boy holds the bridle of the horse at left, perhaps getting ready to start his rounds in the delivery wagon. When Faulstich went out of business, the Price family established a bakery in the storeroom at left and a coffee bar that drew "regulars" for many years. *Photo courtesy of Pearl Price*

MAKING IT CLEAR

The proprietor of the J.W. Rapson Grocery on the corner of W. Williams and Grant Streets spelled it out, clear and bold for his customers: "No credit!" This picture was taken about 1890. Note the separate entrance for customers looking for salt.

AN EARLY 'UNCLE JOE'

Joseph G. Cannon was about to start his third term as representative in Congress from the district that included Danville, his hometown. When this picture was made in 1876, he was 40 years old and had luxuriant red hair and beard.

This was the stately mansion of Joseph G. "Uncle Joe" Cannon, famed Danville congressman and Speaker of the House. Built at a cost of $10,000, the 26-room showplace stood at 418 N. Vermilion Street from 1874 until its demolition in 1946, 20 years after Cannon's death. The site is now a display lot for an automobile dealership.

STATELY MANSION

**DANVILLE ON THE MOVE**

In this 1876 photograph, the Frazier Block of buildings had just been completed from the courthouse alley to Hazel Street but it already had one prestigious tenant--the Vermilion County Bank (later the Second National) had started business at 15 E. Main Street. Dominating the scene, of course, was the new Vermilion County Courthouse, in the final stages of construction at a cost of $105,000. This was probably equivalent to $10.5 million in today's money.

HOME OF THE NEWS

The ground floor of the Vermilion Opera House on the corner of North and Vermilion streets became the home of the Danville *Daily* and *Weekly News* upon its founding in 1873. Published as a morning newspaper, the *News* consolidated with the Danville *Evening Commercial* (founded in 1866) in 1903 to become the modern *Commercial-News*. It was common during that period for daily newspapers to publish a weekly paper as well.

DOUBLE DUTY

The building at 65 W. Main Street did double duty back in 1880 when this photograph was taken. The ground floor was occupied by Yeomans, Shedd and Leseure Hardware Company while the second story was the second location of the *Daily Commercial*. Yeomans and Shedd, as the firm later was known, occupied the location on the corner of Walnut Street until the entire block was razed for urban renewal. Palmer-American National Bank now occupies this and adjacent lots.

John L. Tincher, a Kentuckian, and Joseph G. English, who came to Danville from Perrysville, Indiana, became partners in the Tincher and English grocery store in this building at 15 W. Main Street in 1856. A year later, as assignees of Daniel Clapp, who had closed his stock security bank, they opened the Tincher and English Bank in a one-room log cabin to the east near what is now Redden Square. English became the first president, a position he held for 42 years.

## BIRTH OF A BANK

## STARTLING CHANGE

Nothing illustrates better the startling--and swift--change in downtown Danville's business district than the two photographs above. The top photo shows the old Tincher & English store on W. Main Street, the real birthplace of the First National Bank. This was in 1856. The firm moved to a log cabin on the corner in 1857. But by 1870, as the picture above shows, the bank was solidly in business in a brick building of impressive design and appearance. Note the fancy roof and dormer windows.

## HANDSOME GRADUATE

In the 1880s, graduation from high school usually meant a trip to a professional photographer, at least among leading families. And Clarence Beckwith, younger son of Hiram Beckwith, qualified for this category. As a member of the DHS Class of 1887, he presents a handsome, dignified expression, befitting the grandson of Danville's founder. Watson, Danville's No. 1 photographer at the time, with studios at 18 N. Vermilion Street, utilized the back of the picture for advertising: "Instantaneous portraits of children . . . copies of this cabinet can be had at any time . . . cloudy days as good as sunshine."

## OLD HIGH SCHOOL

This Danville High School building, erected in 1889, was considered the last word from the standpoint of educational facilities and size. But in a few years, a one-story shedlike structure was put up to handle the ever-growing student body. (The students referred to the annex as "the cow shed".) The main entrance, at right, faced W. Seminary Street. The smokestack, at left rear, is on the second Washington School building, erected in 1907. The entrance at the left faces Pine Street.

## EARLY-DAY PRIDE

The first Washington School, built in 1871, was the pride of Danville. The imposing building faced W. Madison Street and was bordered by N. Gilbert Street on the left and Pine Street on the right. The top floor was used as Danville High School until 1889, when a separate building was constructed at the north end of the block, facing Seminary Street. School was serious business in those days; note the absence of a playground!

This was the old Lincoln School, located on W. Williams Street between Chandler and Grant Streets. It was built in 1887 and 1888, serving the elementary-school-age children of an area familiarly known as Tinchertown. It was replaced in 1941, on the same site, by the present building. Tinchertown involved the real estate developed by J.L. Tincher, one of the founders of the First National Bank.

## TINCHERTOWN PRIDE

# FANCY FRONT

It's an elegant display window but it's difficult to tell just what kind of merchandise is being displayed. This was the Brand Building, put up in 1888 on a $2,500 lot at a cost of $9,000. It stood at 51 N. Vermilion Street, the address for many years of Spritz Jewelry Company.

"The more things change, the more they remain the same." Yes, they had this type of establishment back in 1890, too. The Kentucky Liquor Store was advertising an imminent move of location when this photograph was taken. Note that the bystanders are turned away from the camera. The F.W. Woolworth Company store was in this location for many years. The site is now occupied by the annex to the Vermilion County Courthouse, just across Vermilion Street.

## SITE OF MANY CHANGES

## DIVERSIFIED INDUSTRY

The old McMillan and Hill lumber yard stood on the northeast corner of Hazel and North Streets when this 1890 photograph was taken. Later, the Terrace Theater, a popular movie and vaudeville house, was built on the site. An Oakley-Kroger supermarket succeeded the Terrace and now the corner is devoted to a municipal parking lot.

An example of early-day Danville's diversified industry was the Beethoven Organ Factory, with John M. Miller as proprietor. A just-manufactured organ has been placed in the doorway for this photograph, taken some time between 1884 and 1886. Note the drainage ditch, the unpaved roadway and the semi-rural appearance of the neighborhood. This was 529 E. Main Street, a site occupied by the Montgomery Elevator Company today.

The Cooke & Hendricks Store operated at 46 N. Vermilion Street between 1867 and 1895. Judging from the merchandise displayed, it was a genuine variety store, carrying a large inventory. Such stores succeeded if the proprietors were able to guess accurately what their customers wanted.

PRESIDENTIAL 'PALACE'

This was the stately home of Levin T. Palmer, Danville financier and a founder of the Palmer National Bank, as pictured in 1890. It stood on the corner of W. North and N. Gilbert Streets. During World War II, it served as a USO Center, a sort of home-away-from-home for service men, principally those stationed at Chanute Air Force Base in Rantoul, Illinois. It was torn down around 1950 to make way for an A&P Supermarket.

This was the palatial home of Joseph G. English, who was the first president of the First National Bank. Photograph is not dated but probably was taken about 1880. There is no record as to when the dwelling was razed but the site, on the southwest corner of Pine and Harrison Street, has been a vacant lot for more than 50 years.

19TH CENTURY SHOWPLACE

## DIGNIFIED ELEGANCE

The Charles L. English home on N. Vermilion Street became one of Danville's showplaces when it was built in 1880. It stood just north of today's Central Christian Church. Two-and-a-half stories high, it was of brick construction and had galleries at the front and side. Wide, shady front porches, sometimes wrapping around one or more sides, were featured on homes of the era. Note the three chimneys. The home housed the privately-operated Danville Junior College in the early 1930s. The structure was torn down in 1965 to make way for the contemporary Family YMCA.

"Roselawn" was the name Col. R.A. Johnson gave his home at 1620 N. Vermilion and "Roselawn" became the name of the village incorporated around it in the early 20th century. Johnson was an early-day newspaperman, being associated with the Danville *Plain Dealer* in 1866 and later with the Danville *News*, which was founded in 1873. He was Vermilion County coroner in 1898. The home was built in 1867 or 1868. Danville's most elegant apartment building now occupies the site.

### LANDMARK HOME

## THE ROOFTOPS OF DANVILLE

This panoramic photograph of Danville's rooftops was taken about 1875 from the balcony of Lincoln Hall, 14 W. Main Street. In the far background is the old Washington School and in the middle background, center, is the First Presbyterian Church.

## AN EMERGING DOWNTOWN

Business establishments were beginning to flourish downtown as this scene in the unit block of N. Vermilion Street, 1876-1880, would indicate. The new Vermilion County Courthouse, built in 1876, was the pride of Danville residents and the North Street Methodist Church, whose spire rises at the north end of the block, was the most impressive place of worship in the city. Note the stone crosswalks spanning Vermilion and Main Streets; both mule-drawn streetcars and brick paving were still several years in the future.

## BETTER THAN WALKING!

Some of the driver-conductor crews of Danville's first mass transit system pose with their streetcars--and a few of the mules which provided power. The line began operations in 1884 and served until electric streetcars took over in 1892. The building in right background is Heinley's Grand Opera, which started serving the public in 1883. The mules were stabled in the white-painted building at left, later the site of the Palace Theater, now shuttered.

Everything was up-to-date in Danville in 1890, including mass transit. This was the scene looking east on W. Main Street from Franklin Street toward the public square as the mule-drawn streetcar approached. Stone slabs sunk into the roadway at the corners formed walkways to permit pedestrians dry-shod crossing. The old McCormack House, Danville's first hotel, may be seen at extreme left; the three-story building next to it on the corner is the Arlington Hotel. Contemporary Danvilleans remember the Grier-Lincoln Hotel here. The site today is occupied by the drive-in banking complex of the First National Bank.

### MULES AND MUD

FIRST PAVING

Danville streets were being paved with brick in the late 1880s and early 1890s and that's the period when this photograph was taken. The scene is on E. North Street between Hazel and Jackson Streets. Note stacks of brick in background. The workmen are preparing to install curbings of quarried stone.

READY TO ROLL

The finished products of the Danville Carriage Factory are proudly displayed by the men who built them in this photograph, taken some time between 1869 and 1875. The business was located on W. Main Street; after 1900 it was known as the Force Carriage Factory.

## CHANGING TIMES

This was the Bill Unger Harness Shop at 107-111 W. Main Street about 1890. It stood on the site of the McCormack House, Danville's first hotel, built in 1833. The higher building at right was the Arlington Hotel. The entire site is occupied today by the First National's drive-in banking complex.

## THE NEW AND THE OLD

This Huber threshing outfit was the last work in farm "aid" in 1884 but it was being pulled by a team of oxen, a reliable form of power for centuries. The scene is in front of Jackson Wagons and Baker & Holmes machine shop at 45 N. Hazel Street, now a parking lot.

## HOLIDAY HILARITY

The occasion is lost in the mists of history but these fancifully-attired young Danville men must have had a good time. They were photographed on New Year's Day, 1885, possibly following a masked costume ball on New Year's Eve. The man seated center foreground, holding the mask, is identified as H.C. Thomas. Standing immediately behind him is H.D. Thomas and seated immediately to his right, wearing the costume adorned with hearts, is D.D. Gelman. Others in picture are unidentified.

## A TOUCH OF CLASS

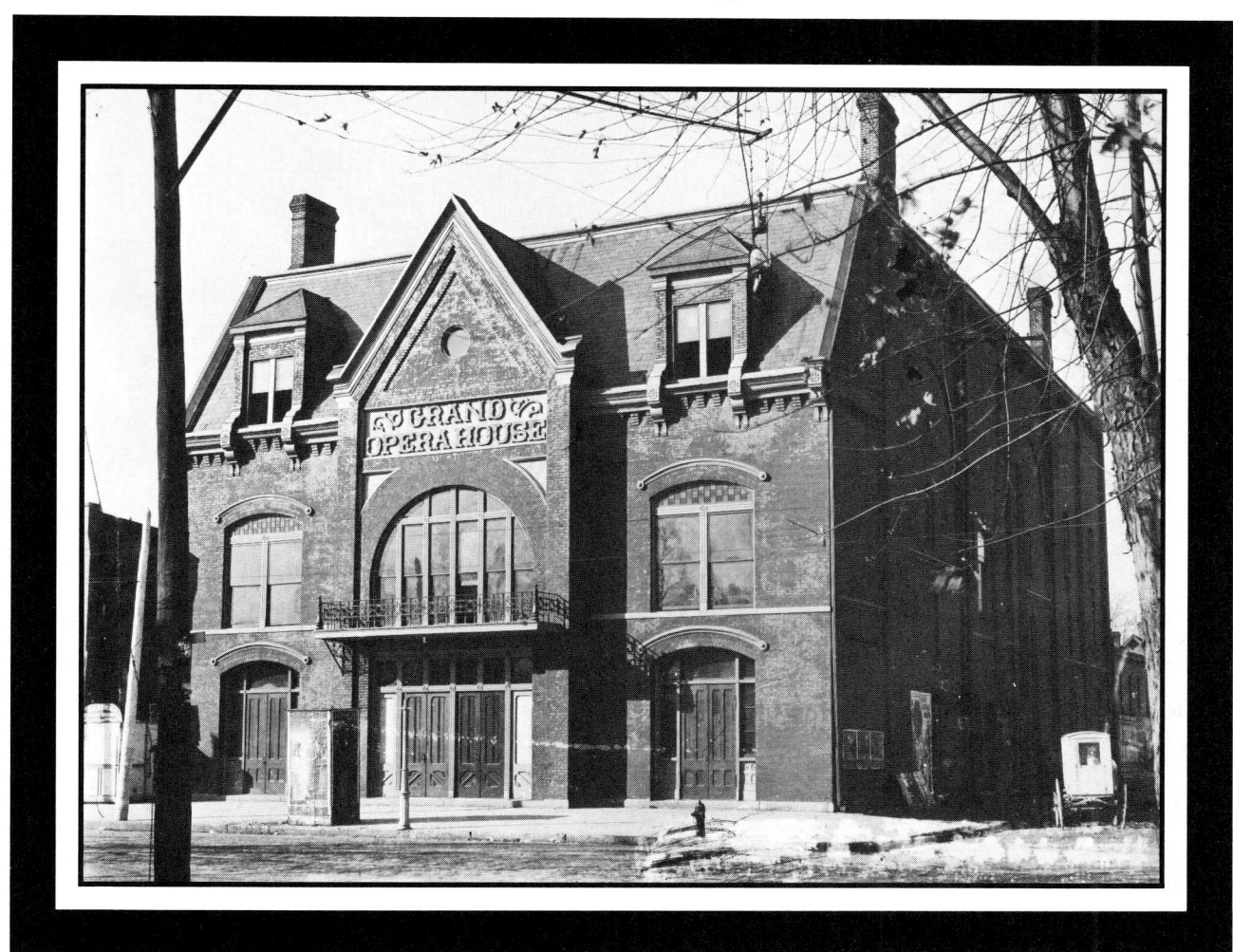

Danville residents felt that culture with a capital "C" had come to their city with the opening of Heinley's Grand Opera House in 1884. For years, the great and near-great of the world of music and theater performed for appreciative audiences in this impressive showhouse. In the early 20th century, it was extensively remodeled and became the Fischer Theater to show movies. It has been closed for several years. Plans to save the historic landmark and restore it to its former glory are uncertain.

No one today knows what the parade was about but the occasion drew a crowd to Danville's public square in 1880. The band, headed by a rider on horseback, is just entering the square from the west on Main Street as pedestrians join people in buggies and wagons to watch and listen. The two-story building in the upper right of the photograph is the First National Bank, then in its 23rd year.

## CHAPTER III

# MORE WARS AND GROWTH

### 1891 - 1920

By 1890, Danville was beginning to move out of the small town class. In the next 10 years it would see its population doubled--to 25,000--the greatest percentage of growth in its history.

What was responsible for this rapid transition to small city status?

The chief factor, undoubtedly, was the railroads. Three lines served the city, connecting Danville with such large population centers--and markets--as Chicago, Indianapolis, St. Louis and Cincinnati. The trains brought in miners and mining equipment, farm machinery and manufactured goods. The trains took out coal and farm products, mostly corn and grain.

Danville was fast becoming a major trading center for a large area of Eastern Illinois and Western Indiana. Its only rivals were Champaign and Urbana, 35 miles west, and Terre Haute, 62 miles across the state line to the southeast. The city actually benefited from the indifferent country roads of the times. A farmer in the Ridge Farm area, for example, had to set aside a full day if he wanted to buy supplies in Danville. It took him four hours each way to drive the 16 miles to "town" in a horse-drawn spring wagon.

But Danville was more than just a place to obtain "store-bought" clothing, staple groceries and new plowshares. It was beginning to take on some of the trappings of much larger places.

For one thing, it was the county seat and as such was where court trials, large and small, were held in the still handsome courthouse which had cost all of $105,000 to build in 1876. These trials, often characterized by fiery exchanges between opposing lawyers, were high theater for townspeople and rural residents alike. The author's grandfather often would take a break from farming so he could attend trials where the colorful Joseph B. Mann was one of the attorneys. Mann was noted for his courtroom theatrics and his rate of success as a defense lawyer.

There were real theaters, too, in the last 10 years of the 19th century, most notably Heinley's Grand Opera, located on the southwest corner of Vermilion and Harrison Streets. It brought to its stage stars of international stature from both New York City and Europe. In later years, it was remodeled and became the Fischer Theater, now shuttered.

In the ultimate decade of the century, Danville took on a modern look, consistent with its larger size and greater importance. Principal streets downtown were paved, thus pulling vehicular traffic and pedestrians alike out of the mud. And the mules which had drawn the streetcars--and were stabled in a barn where the Palace Theater now stands--were put out to pasture, their places usurped by the new electrically-powered cars. In seven years, the new line had 20 cars in operation on 13 miles of track, linking all parts of the city with each other and with the growing downtown business section.

And "growing" is the right word. No longer were stores limited to providing the bare necessities of life. In the 1890s there was a proliferation of millinery shops, dress goods establishments, haberdasheries, restaurants, cigar stores, saloons, music stores, bicycle shops.

Less than three-quarters of a century had passed since the Danville area had been a howling wilderness. But the descendants of the hardy pioneers who had brought civilization here were determined to mix a substantial quantity of fun with the hard reality of making a living.

And have fun they did--joining the rest of the country in a successful search for pleasure that caused historians to dub the decade, "The Gay Nineties." In those days, gay meant only joyous and lively, merry, happy, lighthearted.

Bicycle clubs flourished, giving women for the first time an opportunity to engage in an activity hitherto reserved to men. Separate organizations came into being while at least one was "co-ed." The enormous popularity of the sport was brought about by the invention of the "safety" bicycle, so-called because both wheels were the same diameter, making it much easier to ride and control then the old-fashioned type, with a front wheel that might measure 64 inches in diameter trailed by a rear wheel only a foot high.

The clubs held frequent picnic meetings in good weather and were quite competitive. "Century runs" were popular. A point 50 miles from Danville would be chosen and the contestants would cycle there and back with prizes or trophies awarded for the best times. And some of these times were very good indeed. Speeds of 40 to 50 miles an hour for short distances were not uncommon. On a specially constructed wooden pathway, paralleling the New York Central tracks, an eastern professional rider once paced the *20th Century Limited* for a mile while the famed train maintained a 60-mile-an-hour speed.

More doctors and dentists came to Danville in the 1890s to serve the city's growing medical needs. St. Elizabeth Hospital continued to expand and a second institution came into existence in 1892 to fill the needs of those who wanted a Protestant hospital.

A major boost to Danville's economy came in 1896 with the authorization of a local unit of the National Home for Disabled Volunteer Soldiers. Numerous buildings were erected on the east side of the city and by the end of the century the first of what was to become a veterans' population of 4,000 arrived. Salaries of employees and pension payments of the residents added substantially to the overall income, hence prosperity, of the city.

In the last half of the 1890s, a handsome City Hall was built on Walnut Street and on Main Street, a sturdy stone-arch bridge spanned Stony Creek, effectively opening up the east side of Danville.

And in 1899, a group of Danville businessmen formed the Chamber of Commerce, aimed at enticing industry and business to locate in this city.

The brief Spanish-American War in 1898 caused hardly a ripple in Danville's life. All the men involved were volunteers, chiefly members of the National Guard's Battery A, a light field artilley regiment. Although sent to Puerto Rico, Battery A did not see action; an armistice was declared just as the outfit was preparing to participate in the assault on San Juan.

As midnight, December 31, 1900, ushered in a new year Danville residents greeted 1901--and a new century--with a continuation of the enthusiastic, confident spirit that characterized the closing years of the old.

In the early 1900s, Danvilleans could take pride in the city's progress. The Protestant hospital of 1892 had been renamed the Vermilion County Hospital. And with the building a new structure on Logan Avenue at Fairchild Street, overlooking Horseshoe Lake, it acquired a new name: Lake View Hospital. St. Elizabeth Hospital, too, continued to grow. In the years between 1900 and 1920, downtown Danville took on a great new look with the Temple Building, the Adams Building, the Baum Building, the new Public Library, the federal building and post office, the "skyscraper" 12-story building that housed the First National Bank.

Danville cheered when its "boys" left for France in World War I--and wept when some of them came home in flower-draped caskets.

But despite the somberness of the war, the first two decades ended on an upbeat, confident note. Danville had entered the 20th century with a bang.

## SOLDIERS AT EASE

National Guard troops take their ease in front of the Hotel Annex at Danville Junction in 1894. They had been called into federal service by President Grover Cleveland to maintain order during the great railway strike of that year. Illinois Gov. John Altgeld, although also a Democrat, protested the president's action.

## PEAK COAL PRODUCTION

In 1892, a mine was sunk five miles south of Danville near Westville. At peak production, it mined 2,000 tons a day. This was the first mine in the state to achieve such a large output.

To show how both production and mine employment increased dramatically, one needs to go back to 1883. In that year, Illinois' first annual coal report showed coal mine employment in Vermilion County as 1,061. By 1900, there were nearly three times as many miners--2,706. Coal production during this period increased nearly five-fold--from 416,000 tons annually to 2,030,000 tons. Twice--in 1897 and again in 1899--Vermilion was first among coal-producing counties.

The greatest number of shipping mines in the county was reached in 1890, when 64 were in production.

Old King Coal once was the merriest soul in Vermilion County. And he hired more than "his fiddlers three."

In fact, more men--4,200--were engaged in mining (1901 and again in 1924) than in any other occupation in this century.

Peak production came in 1918. The 3,971,330 tons produced were almost twice the amount for 1900 (2,003,730 tons).

From the turn of the century through the closing year of World War I, coal mining reached its highest point. Output for the nation quadrupled.

The railroads were important to the mines in the Danville district, purchasing approximately 27 percent of all they produced.

## TWO-HORSEPOWER CAB

John Noone, who was Danville's premier liveryman at the turn of the century, is in the driver's seat with his little daughter in this 1899 photograph. Cabs did a thriving business; there were 40 passenger trains in and out of Danville daily at the time, most of them at the old Danville Junction.

This summer scene of the fountain on the grounds of the Soldiers Home, sometime before 1910, shows why the beautifully landscaped government reservation had become a Danville showplace in a matter of a few short years; two decades before, this had been nothing but farmland on the eastern edge of the city. The fountain is gone but the bandstand, at right, where free public concerts were played almost daily by the Soldiers Home band in good weather, remains.

### A CITY SHOWPLACE

### SOLDIERS HOME

Its official name was Danville Branch, National Home for Disabled Volunteer Soldiers. But to residents of Danville it soon became the Old Soldiers Home or just the Soldiers Home.

Opened for use in 1898, the home had a 1900 population of 1,583. At one time, 4,000 veterans lived there. The cost of buildings, land and permanent improvements: $1,195,617. It is interesting to note that its land area of 324.56 acres is less than 60 acres smaller than that of the principality of Monaco.

It is not true that "Uncle Joe" Cannon owned the land and sold it to the government. The principal owners were the Noone and Olehy families: all the owners received a combined total of $45,961.

In recent years the actual size of the government reservation has diminished inasmuch as considerable land was given to Danville Area Community College (DACC) for a campus, along with a number of buildings declared surplus by the General Service Administration of the federal government. Title to this property was conveyed to the college by an act of Congress. The late Senator Paul Douglas, D-Ill., was the principal sponsor of the legislation which accomplished the transfer.

# FIRST OFFICERS

1. Colonel Isaac Clements
   Governor
2. Major Martin J. Barger
   Treasurer
3. Major Daniel C. Jones
   Surgeon
4. Captain Edward B. Wheeler
   Quartermaster
5. Captain John W. Newlon
   Commissary of Subsistence
6. Rev. Melchior Auer
   Chaplain

These were the first officers of Danville's Soldiers Home. All had served in the Civil War and held military titles. The home operated as a military establishment. Army rules and regulations were observed generally and residents wore uniforms with a military cut, blue in color originally but khaki later. Col. Clements' civilian title was governor.

## LAZY, HAZY DAYS OF SUMMER

Boating and picnicking, two pleasant pastimes of summer, are enjoyed in this scene from the turn of the century at Danville's Soldiers Home. Residents and their guests hover around picnic tables in the grove while others skim over the surface of Lake Franklin. The lake was renamed Lake Clements, in honor of the home's first governor, and eventually was drained. A nine-hole golf course was built on the lake bed and provides recreation for patients and staff.

### AN IMPORTANT SERVICE

Livery stables performed a vital service in Danville prior to the coming of the automobile. They stabled and fed travelers' horses, housed their wagons or carriages overnight, provided taxi service, rented riding or driving horses (with accompanying conveyances). In this 1910 photograph, G.L. McClellan, proprietor, is the man in the white shirt holding the reins of two horses. His establishment stood on the southeast corner of S. Vermilion and South Streets.

## CONTROVERSIAL IMPROVEMENT

Danville residents had mixed emotions about their new City Hall in 1896 during the administration of Mayor John Beard. While they liked its looks, they thought the cost--$30,000--was too high and they grumbled because the stone came from a quarry the mayor owned. First floor housed police headquarters, the holdover for city prisoners, and the police magistrate's courtroom. Second floor held the council chamber and offices and meeting rooms for aldermen, later city commissioners. The building and adjoining Central Fire Station, smaller building at right, served until present City Building was erected on Hazel Street in 1954. The house at left was torn down to make way for the Salvation Army Citadel in 1925. The west side of block between Main and North Streets now is occupied by First National Bank drive-in banking complex and the municipal parking garage.

## HANDSOME STRUCTURE

The Odd Fellows Building at 125 N. Vermilion Street was one of the more handsome structures downtown as this photograph, taken before 1900, attests. Later, Woodbury Book Company occupied the first floor, where it remains to this day. The building virtually was destroyed by fire in 1914 and had to be rebuilt.

# LONG SPAN, SHORT LIFE

The old Red Bridge connected Danville and South Danville, spanning the Vermilion River which hitherto had to be crossed by ferry. It served from 1857 until it was replaced by an iron bridge in 1895. But ever-increasing traffic made it unacceptable in a little more than 25 years; it was replaced by the first Memorial Bridge in 1923. That span, in turn, was succeeded by the present Memorial Bridge some 30 years later.

This stone-arch bridge carrying Main Street over Stony Creek played a significant role in the late 19th century development of Danville. Built by John Beard in 1895, it opened up the east side of the city by providing an improved access to the center city. Beard, a stone mason, quarry owner, ice merchant, newspaper proprietor and three-time mayor of Danville, is credited with a remarkable feat of engineering in the design and construction of the sandstone bridge. The segmental arch design, or flatter arch, required complex engineering and masonry skills. Beard "overbuilt" the span by using heavier stone than necessary, which may explain why the span endured. The state highway department wanted to tear it down in 1984 and replace it but a determined fight by local history buffs succeeded in having it placed on the National Register of Historic Places. The state now will strengthen the bridge by building an arch within the original arch. The span carries 16,000 vehicles daily.

## SIGNIFICANT SPAN

## COMFORT NO OBJECT

This dashing young soldier was Sgt. Joseph J. Smith of Danville's Battery A, which saw service but no combat in Puerto Rico during the Spanish-American War. Smith was 20 years old when this photograph was taken in 1898. He lived to be past 90 and for many years was proprietor of a flower shop on the northeast corner of Vermilion and North Streets known as Smith the Florist.

The choke-collar tunic worn by Col. Phil Yeager of Danville obviously was not intended for the comfort of the wearer but it was in vogue clear up to the end of World War I. Yeager, a contractor in civilian life, was a captain with this city's Battery A, Field Artillery, in the Spanish-American War.

It seemed that all of Danville was on hand on a day in late spring, 1898, to bid a fond farewell to members of Battery A, about to entrain for service in the Spanish-American War. This was the scene at the Wabash Railroad crossing of E. Main Street. Guns on the flatcars are Hotchkiss light artillery pieces. Troops first went to Camp Butler in Springfield, Illinois, then to Camp George Thomas, Chickamauga, Georgia, for two months' training before embarking for Puerto Rico. They were ready to engage the enemy when a cease-fire ended hostilities. The old passenger station can be seen at right, above tops of passenger coaches. The turreted building in left background is the Illinois Hotel, built in 1895, at the corner of Washington Avenue and Van Buren Street.

## HANDSOME SOLDIER

## THEY ALL TURNED OUT

# HEYDAY OF THE STREET CAR

"Clang, clang, clang went the trolley!
"Ding, ding, ding went the bell!"

These words from *The Trolley Song* conjure a time when Americans were rapidly discarding the old ways, enthusiastically putting on the new. Then, as now, there was eagerness to do things better, faster, cheaper. Electricity was the means to accomplish many of these ends; in fact, the compulsion that created the modern "live better electrically" slogan was just as evident, in proportion to what was available.

One thing available was the electric streetcar and Danville took advantage of it. And so on September 2, 1892, the literal horsepower (or mule power) that pulled cars gave way to something better.

The day before had been the anniversary of another milestone in Danville's progress. It was on September 1, 1873, that William P. and Joseph G. Cannon had started the Vermilion County Bank, chartered in 1881 as the Second National Bank. The dates may have been coincidental but there was a close connection between the business origins; the men who had started the bank also were behind the Danville Street Railway and Light Company.

Streetcars for Danville were in tune with the times. Between 1890 and 1900, decade of the city's greatest growth, the population increased 100 percent--to 25,000. By 1899, the street railway system operated 20 cars on 13 miles of track. The car barn was on the site of the Palace Theater, now shuttered.

Danville's acceptance of streetcar service was rapid. Soon the tracks extended to the city limits on the north and to the Soldiers Home (which began building as the century ended) on the east.

The C&EI Shops were served by the Oaklawn line that turned off Main Street at Illinois Street and ended at Oregon Street.

The E. Fairchild Street line went beyond the Fairgrounds to Michigan Avenue.

Midtown was served by the Junction and Douglas Park cars.

The Lincoln Park run was up Madison Street to Chandler, thence to Fairchild Street and ending at Lake View Hospital.

Other lines were on E. English Street to the Springhill Cemetery gates; on W. English Street to Logan Avenue; to Grape Creek with near connection to the Douglas Park car, and to Vermilion Heights.

It was a short ride from downtown to his home at 418 N. Vermilion Street but "Uncle Joe" Cannon often took it. Fact was that Cannon Alley, just south of the big mansion, was a regular car stop.

In 1903, the McKinley System, well on its way to becoming the giant among Midwestern traction systems, bought the Cannon interests.

Although the Grape Creek and E. English Street runs were abandoned and the Heights service taken over by the interurban, the streetcar system reached a height of prosperity in the early 1920s. Trackage was approximately 21 miles and there were 72 regular runs daily.

The prosperity was short-lived. With the rapid increase in automobiles, the street cars days were numbered. Buses had been put on N. Gilbert Street (which never had been served by streetcars) in 1926, the year "Uncle Joe" died. And then on December 14, 1936, the end came to a glorious era...

This picture symbolizes the heyday of the streetcar in Danville. Taken about 1913, it shows No. 145, one of four cars of the same type purchased second-hand a few years before in Washington, D.C. A double-end, double-truck car, it was 39 feet long, could seat 40 passengers. Note the "Soldiers Home" sign on the car. J.R. Gritton, who died in 1952, is the motorman; with him in the front of the car and wearing the straw hat is the late E.J. Horner, the assistant superintendent, who was to succeed his boss, the late Mike Connor. The conductor (on rear step) is unidentified.

## MAMMOTH REVIVAL

Billy Sunday, the major league ballplayer-turned evangelist, held the largest revival in Danville's history in this frame tabernacle in 1910. The frame building, which held 10,000, was built for the occasion in Williams Pasture, just east of where Danville High School now stands. The fiery Sunday often smashed a full set of china dinnerware during a sermon to emphasize his points. A 500-voice choir sang for the services.

---

This view of the east side of the public square shows four principal ways we got around Danville back in 1900. Two of the one-man streetcars are seen on the single-track line as pedestrians walk around the courthouse. On the right, a horse and buggy stand at the curb while near the center of the picture a man rides an old-fashioned high-wheel bicycle.

## THE WAY WE GOT AROUND

# EARLY FEMINIST

Lucy Woodbury, daughter of Dr. W.W.R. Woodbury, Danville druggist and friend of Abraham Lincoln, was an early believer that a woman could do anything a man could do—often better. She was an enthusiastic cyclist and a member of the League of American Wheelmen, as a copy of her membership card for 1893 attests. Many women belonged to the national organization but none would have dreamed of suggesting a name change to "League of American Wheelpersons."

## LADIES CYCLED, TOO

With the advent of the "safety" bicycle (front and back wheels were the same diameter), cycling became a very popular pastime, with girls and women taking it up enthusiastically. The first Lady Cycling Club in Danville was organized in 1890 and members, joined by a few male friends, posed for this picture in front of the new (1889) Danville High School building at Seminary, Pine and Gilbert Streets. In the picture, front seated, left to right: Tine Peyton, Sophie Andros and Mrs. L.A. McLouth; at back, Bertha Peyton, Rose Parker, Flo Woodbury, A.G. "Gardie" Woodbury, her brother; George Gordon, Millie McKee, Lucy Woodbury, Flo's sister, Belle Dale and Gen Wright, extreme right.

## ATTRACTIVE INTERIOR

This picture probably was taken in 1904, when the Danville Public Library opened to patrons, 21 years after its humble beginning in rented quarters on W. Main Street. The so-called "delivery room" is dominated by the huge marble-faced desk, where books were checked out to patrons and checked in when they were returned. The library was enlarged greatly by a sizeable addition to the rear of the building, constructed in the late 1920s. Today's library is figuratively bursting at the seams; triple the present floor space is needed to provide adequate service for the remainder of this century.

## LIBRARY'S THIRD STOP

After a six-year stay on the second floor of a building at 132-134 N. Vermilion Street, the Danville Public Library moved to its third location in 1901: Upstairs in the building located on the northeast corner of Walnut and North streets. The next stop would be its very own hansome home.

## LASTING LANDMARK

This is the way the Danville Public Library looked in 1904, shortly after completion of construction. And its exterior today has much the same appearance. Andrew Carnegie, the philanthropist steel baron, made grants to communities across the nation for the building of libraries; Danville, Ridge Farm and the Soldiers Home were the beneficiaries in Vermilion County. Expansion of space in the 1920s and modernization in recent years have been at the rear and have not detracted from the facility's impressive charm of architecture. The library is on the National Register of Historic Places and cannot be capriciously torn down or used for other than library purposes.

## CHILDREN'S ANGEL

Laura Lee was described by Historian Katherine Stapp as "... one of the great humanitarians of Danville history." To countless children with no homes of their own, she was a special angel.

Mrs. Lee, a teacher, began her mission of mercy by asking, and receiving from the court, custody of some children who were about to be sent to reform school for lack of a proper home.

From this start, Mrs. Lee expanded her self-imposed obligation of love. She and her husband, Elias, took more children into their home, moving to a larger house because "their kids" needed more room.

Inspired by her selflessness, the community rallied to her support, donating clothing, food and money. Later, the county provided per capita funds. Mrs. Lee supplemented this money by giving street carnivals and cake walks, raising funds to remodel her home for the ever-growing "family" she was acquiring with every trip to court.

She was in her 57th year when she died but her husband carried on the work she started.

Today, a fine community center on E. Williams Street is known as the Laura Lee Fellowship House. It's a fitting tribute to a lady who labored so long and effectively for others.

But the greatest tribute probably lies unspoken in the hearts of hundreds of children, now adults, who received a great gift of love because of a kind and compassionate woman back in 1915.

## MORE THAN A LAWYER

Arthur Hall was a lawyer and a good one. He also was a skillful, impartial and just judge of the Vermilion County Probate Court. A quiet man, he sometimes was referred to jokingly, but always with respect, as "Silent Art." He was a standout football player at the University of Illinois and was named to the U. of I.'s Hall of Fame. As a part-time grid coach after graduation (serving without pay), he master-minded the Illini to their only perfect season—undefeated, untied, unscored upon. He was a lifelong advocate of hard roads, drew up the plans for a system of all-weather roads in Vermilion County and worked to get a bond issue referendum passed. Of all his honors he may have been proudest of his image as "the man who pulled Vermilion County out of the mud."

INDUSTRIALIST

Julius Hegeler Sr. came to Danville and founded the Hegeler Zinc Company in 1905. Located south of the city, the plant expanded to become a major economic factor, employing several hundred, and shipping its product to all parts of the nation. At one time it had its own coal mine. The site and some of the buildings today are occupied by the Peterson/Puritan Company.

RESTAURANT TYCOON

John R. Thompson was born in 1865 near Fithian, lived in Danville before moving to Chicago and became involved in restaurant operation about the time of the 1893 World's Fair. Thompson Restaurants featured cafeteria service, with the customer taking food to a chair whose one arm flared into a table-like surface. Danville had one of his restaurants, located on the west side of Vermilion Street's unit block. By 1903, Thompson had 10 restaurants but this was just the beginning. Located in the eastern half of the United States, Thompson restaurants ultimately could be found from Canada to Georgia. The Vermilion County native married a daughter of Georgetown Civil War hero George Washington Holloway and their descendants operate restaurants today under the name of Holloway House.

### ELDER ELITE

Joseph G. "Uncle Joe" Cannon was in the twilight years of his long and distinguished career in the House of Representatives when he took four of his Danville cronies for a ride. Seated in the back of his Locomobile touring car in this June, 1914, photograph are, from left, Cannon, R.D. McDonald, entrepreneur and real estate developer, W.R. Jewell, newspaperman and postmaster longer than anyone in local history, Joseph Mann, colorful defense lawyer, and Gen. John C. Black, Danville's outstanding hero of the Civil War. At the wheel is Lester "Red" Morris, Uncle Joe's chauffeur for many years. In background is the brand-new Elks Club, now the site of a used car display lot across the alley from Danville Public Library.

'THE HOUSE WILL BE IN ORDER'

Danville's "Uncle Joe" Cannon presides as speaker of the U.S. House of Representatives, a position he held between 1903 and 1911. Note the gavel in his left hand. Unlike some southpaw pitchers, however, "Uncle Joe" had well-nigh perfect control of the House during his tenure.

## CANNON

Cannon was elected speaker of the House in 1903, succeeding David B. Henderson of Iowa. Blair Bolles, his biographer, described him as the "Tyrant from Illinois" in a book of that title. Congressional historians have assessed Cannon as the most powerful House speaker in U.S. history. For example, he appointed all members, both Republican and Democrat, to all 62 House committees.

During the eight years of his tenure, no bills came out of committee without his blessing. Bolles said that Cannon extended his influence to the Senate, also Republican-controlled, and became virtual dictator of the United States.

Cannon's political philosophy today would be described as right-wing conservative. He believed that the less government

By the late 1890s, Rep. Joseph G. Cannon Illinois had become one of the powerful leaders of the Republican-dominated House of Representatives. He was so influential that President William McKinley summoned him to the White House and asked him to sponsor and quietly steer through Congress a $50 million dollar appropriation bill for arms and munitions. The President was convinced that war with Spain was imminent but wanted to avoid stirring up the country by his personal involvement in defense legislation.

the better off the nation. This concept put him on a collision course with President Theodore Roosevelt and could have cost him a chance at the White House. In 1908, "T.R." backed William Howard Taft, who was elected.

In 1911, progressive Republicans, led by George Norris of Nebraska, plotted a successful parliamentary coup that stripped Cannon of most of his autocratic powers.

But earlier in his reign as speaker, Cannon was very popular. He was known to his colleagues (as well as his Danville constituents) as "Uncle Joe" and they gave him a lavish 70th birthday party in 1906.

In Danville—and, in fact, the whole Illinois 18th Congressional District—"Uncle Joe" was virtually invincible. He first was elected to the House in 1872, while living in Tuscola, Illinois (he moved to Danville the following year and built the mansion in 1874) and for the next 50 years was re-elected every two years except for 1890 and in the Democratic landslide of 1912. His last election was in 1920; his farewell appearance in the House was early in 1923. He thus was elected 23 times and served 46 years, among the longest tenures of any U.S. representative or senator.

One of three House office buildings is named in his honor.

## IROQUOIS THEATER TRIAL

The nation's attention was focused on Danville in 1907 when one of the biggest trials in the county's history was held.

Reporters and photographers from many of the country's largest newspapers crowded into the city for the trial of Will J. Davis, manager of the Iroquois Theater in Chicago.

Davis was being tried for manslaughter in the death of Veva Jackson, one of the 596 persons who perished in the fire and resulting panic at the theater on December 30, 1903. A change of venue had brought the case here from Cook County.

More than 200 witnesses and some of the country's top legal talent also were on hand. The prosecution's team included Cook County Assistant State's Attorney J.J. Barbour, Vermilion County State's Attorney John W. Keeslar and George Buckingham in Chicago.

The defense was represented by Levy Mayer, Alfred Austrian and W.J. Calhoun, all of Chicago, and Joseph B. Mann, noted Danville attorney. Calhoun, who later became minister to China, was a former law partner of Mann in Danville.

Firemen and policemen involved in the blaze were among the witnesses slated to testify. Hundreds of exhibits for the prosecution had been brought to Danville and stored in an express company office.

Presiding judge was E.R.E. Kimbrough.

A jury was selected with some difficulty and the first witness, Mrs. M.C. Jackson, mother of the young fire victim, was called.

The defense, however, immediately challenged the validity of the Chicago fire ordinance, on the violation of which the manslaughter charge was based. It was contended that the word "large" used to describe buildings covered in the ordinance was indefinite. Attorneys also claimed that Davis, as resident manager of the theater, was not responsible for the violation.

A legal battle between prosecution and defense ensued. To prove his point, Mayer brought in volumes and volumes of law books which had been carefully researched.

Prior to the change of venue, Judge Marcus Kavanaugh of Chicago had upheld the validity of the ordinance.

Finally, on March 9, 1907, the sixth day of the trial, Judge Kimbrough overruled Kavanaugh's decision and held the ordinance invalid. The jury was directed to return a verdict of not guilty and Davis was freed.

---

## FROM MULES TO MOVIES

Back in 1884, this was the site of the barn which housed the mules that pulled Danville's first streetcars. When the mules were put out to pasture after the electric streetcars made their appearance, the building was remodeled and in 1907 became the Lyric Theater. Both motion pictures and stage productions were the attraction here and later the name was changed to the Palace. The theater is still there but has been shuttered for several years. The building at extreme right was the Heinley Grand Opera building, which opened its doors in 1883. It, too, was remodeled and became the Fischer Theater, also boarded up.

## KING OF THE CARNIVALS

In this 1900 photograph, the C.A. Wortham Carnival is shown unloading at the Wabash Freight House south of Main Street. Wortham was a Vermilion County native and was known as the carnival king, having several shows on the road at the same time. He died in 1933 and is buried in Springhill Cemetery. For years, carnival people made pilgrimages to his grave whenever they played Danville.

### RAIL BIRDS CHEER 'EM ON

Rail birds give vocal encouragement to their favorites as they watch the finish of this harness race at the Ellsworth Park track in 1909. The track was situated on the west side of the park and gave way to the first municipal golf course in Illinois.

## SHOOT THE CHUTES

Young fry, in search of a thrill at the turn of the century, begged their parents to take them to Wonderland Park, located at the south edge of Danville. Principal attraction was the roller-coaster ride, at left in picture but there also were other carnival-type rides and a carousel. Wonderland Park was situated on the west side of S. Gilbert Street just north of the intersection with the Tilton Road. The photograph was taken between 1903 and 1905.

## CITY'S 'OLD SWIMMING HOLE'

The North Fork River through Ellsworth Park was the city's popular "old swimming hole" in the early days of the century as this 1909 photograph suggests. Low white building at river's edge was the bathhouse; the park pavilion is higher on the bank. The river bed was somewhat treacherous, marked by several stepoffs, and several drownings and near-drownings occurred over the years. There has been no provision for swimming at the park in modern times.

# THE INTERURBAN

Interurban car service was an important part of the passenger transportation picture in Danville in the early part of the 20th century.

William B. McKinley (no relation to the president) of Champaign-Urbana was a traction baron who held properties throughout downstate Illinois. In 1901, he bought the Danville Street Railway System and began building the far-flung Illinois Traction System, later, the Illinois Terminal Railroad.

The first service from the city was to Tilton and Westville. To carry the lines south, McKinley built a high trestle across the Vermilion River. Service soon was extended to Georgetown and Ridge Farm. Later a line was built to Oakwood, Fithian, Homer and eventually to Urbana-Champaign. To accommodate this line, a bridge was built over the North Fork River in Ellsworth Park circa 1910-12.

Next, McKinley extended service to Springfield and, finally, to St. Louis, Missouri, spending $4 million of his own funds to build a bridge across the Mississippi River. A branch line from Peoria joined the main line and provided overnight sleeper car service to St. Louis.

The station for both city streetcars and the interurban line was 2-4 W. Main Street on the public square until 1923 when the Illinois Power and Light Company (now Illinois Power Company) took control of the Danville Street Railway and Light Company and built a building on S. Vermilion Street. The north half of that structure was the passenger station for interurban service and also housed the Postal Telegraph office. The utility bought the interurban line from Illinois Traction Company in 1927, gradually cut back service and abandoned the Georgetown line in 1936. The power company moved out of the business in 1945 but the new owner, Illinois Terminal Railroad, continued to provide passenger service until April, 1952.

A BRIDGE THAT WAS

This was the Illinois Traction Company (later, the Illinois Terminal Railroad) bridge over the North Fork River south of Ellsworth Park about 1912. Much larger interurban cars were in use in later years. The Ellsworth Park dam backed up the river to create a swimming beach that was very popular in the 1920s and 1930s, although several drownings and near-drownings occurred there over the years.

## THRILLING RIDE

Interurban passengers to Tilton, Westville, Georgetown or Ridge Farm rocked and swayed over the Vermilion River bridge and approach trestle. They could look out a window and see nothing but river or ground 40 to 50 feet below. But no car ever jumped the track or stalled half-way across. The bridge-trestle was dismantled in the 1940s and the metal used in the war effort. This photograph was taken in 1911, with the car headed north from South Danville.

In 1905, Danville was moving in many directions. The Plaza Hotel, at right, was considered one of the finest hostelries in Illinois outside Chicago. The public square was paved with brick and the streetcar line (tracks in foreground) had been electrified for 13 years. Moreover, William McKinley's Illinois Traction System, which had started in Danville, had extended its lines to serve Westville, Georgetown and Ridge Farm. The cars in this picture on S. Vermilion Street and making the turn off W. Main Street would be supplanted later by much larger standard railroad-size self-propelled coaches. The building at left in the picture was the interurban passenger station until 1923.

## CITY ON THE MOVE

## WHEN THE ELEPHANTS RAN AWAY

"The elephants are loose!"

This cry echoing through Danville on a spring day in 1910, signaled the start of one of the wildest safaris in the annals of the American circus.

The Commercial-News of Wednesday, April 27, 1910, carried the story in a prominent three-column spread on Page 1. The banner line read: EIGHT ELEPHANTS ESCAPE FROM CIRCUS AND GO ON RAMPAGE.

Here is how the reporter saw it:

"Eight of the elephants with the Ringling show stampeded late Wednesday afternoon and for nearly an hour were at large while a dozen keepers and other showmen who are acquainted with the habits of elephants went after them.

"Shortly before 3 o'clock, as the elephants were being unloaded from their cars near the Big Four freight house, Gilbert Street and the railroad, one of the pachyderms made a break and before the remainder could be quieted, eight had escaped.

"After gaining their liberty, the big fellows scattered.

"Two of the pachyderms going north caused the team of Barney O'Neal to run away, breaking the wagon and injuring the team.

"Two elephants were captured together near Lincoln Park, a third was caught in the alley between Harmon Avenue and Robinson Street just north of Clay. Others were caught on Chandler Street north of Woodbury, while one was captured on Ann Street and another on Payne Avenue."

The dash to freedom was led by a female elephant named Satan. She was caught on Hungrey Hollow road Wednesday night.

Satan's role as troublemaker cost her her life. The next day she was taken in a railroad car to near Lyons Yards. Under circus supervision, a block-and-falls gallows was rigged. With 100 men pull-on the ropes, she was strangled.

Although Ringling put on performances the following day, Thursday, the circus' troubles were far from over. Claim agents settled a multitude of small claims totaling around $2,000.

Altogether, the affair cost Ringling around $30,000, including the $15,000 value of Satan and the expense of re-breaking the runaways.

It was a day long to be remembered . . . the day the elephants ran away.

### ON A REAL 'TEAR'

When circus elephants went on a rampage on the west side of Danville, back in 1910, they showed little respect for houses, gardens, lawns—or even washing hanging on the line, as this artist's conception illustrates. Circus claim agents paid one lady $15 for "large washing destroyed."

### DINNER IS SERVED

In 1900, Dalbey's Restaurant was at 57 N. Vermilion Street, a good spot to attract trade. The Dalbey brothers pose for this picture, probably on opening day. It's to be hoped that the chef was more skillful than the sign painter!

TOPS AMONG THEATERS

Built in 1907 as the Airdrome, the Terrace, as it quickly was renamed, was Danville's largest as well as most imposing theater for more than 20 years. Many stars of the vaudeville circuit appeared on its stage and the first sound motion picture, *Show Girl,* starring Al Jolson and Alice White, was shown there in 1928. Simply too big to be profitable, it was torn down in the early 1930s to make way for a grocery supermarket. The site, at the northeast corner of Hazel and North Streets, is now a municipal parking lot. The building at right with a smokestack is the Webster Grocer Company.

FOR MAN AND BEAST

Salisbury and Jamison sold groceries and feed (and just about everything else in their store in South Danville on what is now S. Gilbert Street) as a sign in the window proclaims. In this 1905 picture, from left, are Tom Salisbury, one of the partners and father-in-law of Cal Jamison, who operated the store until his death in 1946; four-year-old Danny Jamison, who grew up to be Dr. Jamison, a practicing physician in Wheaton, Illinois; Oppie Hall; Ed Goulding, and Dr. James B. Hundley. Man at right, a customer, is William Dunsworth. Mr. Jamison's daughter, Disa Maxwell, operated the store until its closing in 1967.

HUMBLE BEGINNING

This was the humble beginning of today's magnificent Lakeview Medical Center. Known at first as the Protestant Hospital Association of Vermilion County, formed in 1892, it began operations in 1894 in this remodeled dwelling, located on E. Fairchild Street at Washington Avenue, across from present-day Danville High School. There was no elevator.

In less than 30 years from its estabishment in 1882 in a converted home, St. Elizabeth Hospital had grown to this impressive size in 1910. Such progress indirectly was responsible for the establishment of what was to become Lake View Hospital across town in 1894. Although members of all denominations were welcomed as patients, St. Elizabeth was run by the Catholic order of Sisters of St. Francis of the Sacred Heart. Some residents felt they would be more at ease in a Protestant institution and that inspired the effort to obtain a second hospital.

CONTINUING TO GROW

## CENTER FOR HEALING

After 18 months on E. Fairchild Street (at a rental cost of $200 per year), the predecessor of today's Lakeview Medical Center moved to the present site and erected this handsome brick building, capable of accommodating 40 to 45 patients—at a charge of one dollar a day. The cost of the building and 5½ acres of grounds was $16,500. The name was changed to the Vermilion County Protestant Hospital Association.

## LAKEVIEW

The history of Lakeview Medical Center goes back 95 years—to December 1, 1892, when a charter issued by the state of Illinois was filed with the Vermilion County recorder.

The name of the corporation was listed as the "Protestant Hospital Association of Danville, Illinois." The "object for which it is formed is to build and maintain a Protestant hospital for the care and relief of sick and wounded persons."

The first patients were accepted in July, 1894, in a former private dwelling that had been remodeled. This stood on E. Fairchild Street across from Williams pasture, later the site of the present Danville High School building. The hospital paid $200 a year rent. It could accommodate up to 20 patients but only averaged 10 to 11. There was no elevator.

After 18 months at the E. Fairchild Street location, the hospital association bought five acres of land on the west side of Logan Avenue, stretching from W. Fairchild Street to the entrance of the old tuberculosis sanitarium. The cost was $1,500.

A brick building was constructed at a cost of $15,000. Opened in 1896, it was capable of caring for 40 to 45 patients. (A patient was charged $1 a day!)

After the move to the new building, the hospital's name was changed to Vermilion County Protestant Hospital Association. This was confused with the Vermilion County Home, colloquially referred to as "the poor farm," so the name was changed again in 1903 to Lake View Hospital, inspired by Horseshoe Lake, north of the hospital on land owned by Inter-State Water Company.

In 1916, the Minta Harrison wing was added to the south end of the building, increasing bed capacity to 125 patients. John Harrison, publisher and principal owner of the *Commercial-News* at the time, donated $200,000 to the hospital for the addition in memory of his mother.

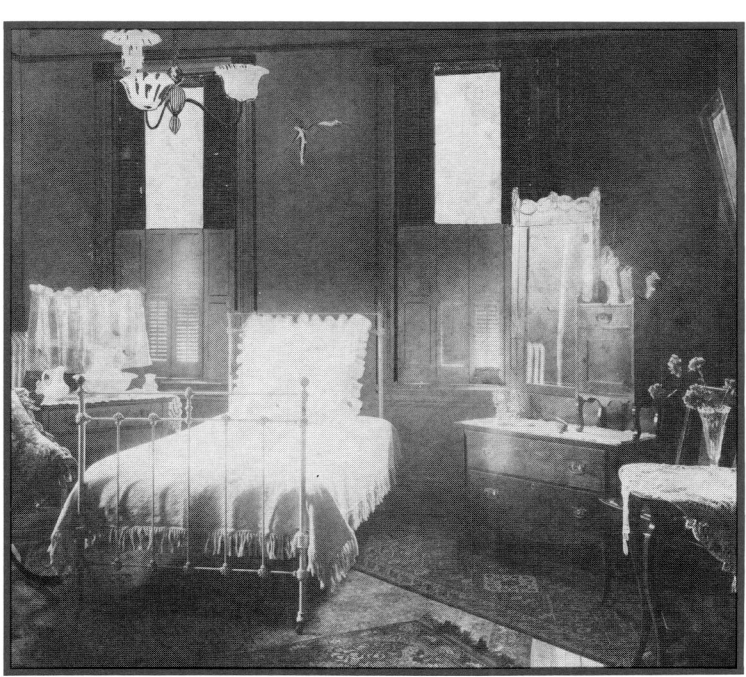

The bed didn't change contours at the press of a power button but it did look comfortable. This was the home-like interior of a private room in the new brick building which housed the fore-runner of Lakeview Medical Center around the turn of the century.

## COMFORTS OF HOME

## FIRST AUTOMOBILE IN DANVILLE

This German-made Benz horseless carriage stopped overnight in Danville on May 24, 1896, on its way from Decatur to Indianapolis, Indiana. Hundreds of bicycle riders escorted the car into town and thousands were on the street to greet it. No one then could dream that in less than a hundred years approximately 40,000 motor vehicles would be registered in the city. The trip between Decatur and Danville took nine hours.

## 'AUTOMOBUBBLING, YOU AND I . . .'

These words from a popular song of the day seem appropriate for this 1900 picture of horseless carriages lined up for the first run of the Danville Auto Club. These early-day cars had bodies similar to buggies, rolled on bicycle-type tires and were steered by tillers (the steering wheel was still some years in the future). Members of the Holmes family were automobile enthusiasts from the beginning as the photograph indicates.

## PROUD MOMENT

Otto Everett, at right, poses proudly beside his 1917 Model-T Ford with his son, Fred. Otto emigrated from Germany to the United States in 1880 with his parents, Fritz and Caroline Everett, a younger brother, Frederich, and two sisters. The family settled in Danville and the men became coal miners. The family home still stands—the first house east of the fire station on Perrysville Avenue, now occupied by son Karl Everett.
*Photo courtesy of Elsie (Everett) Marshall*

## HOW CARS HAVE CHANGED!

Don Willard of the Allith-Prouty Company, hardware manufacturers, came to Danville in 1912 and shortly afterward bought that year's model of the American Underslung automobile, manufactured in Indianapolis, Indiana. Note the flaring front fenders, huge wheels, hinged windshield. With Willard in the picture is his daughter. Now deceased, Willard became president of Allith-Prouty, continued to work past age 90 and described himself as "the oldest working mechanical engineer in the United States."

James A. Meeks, a Danville lawyer, sits proudly in his first automobile, a 1912 Haines touring car. Note steering wheel on right side and the tool box mounted on the running board. Twenty years later he was elected to Congress on the Democratic ticket and served six years in the House of Representatives. Other people in the car, including the driver, are unidentified although the woman in the rear seat probably was Meeks' wife, Frances Pearson Meeks, noted in her own right as an educator. She was the daughter of Gustavus Pearson, who made a fortune in mercantile trade following the gold strike in California.

## HIS FIRST CAR

# BEFORE AND AFTER

Nothing illustrates better the importance of all-weather roads than these "before and after" scenes of the Georgetown Road south of Danville. Top picture shows the muddy, rutted half-frozen road surface during the winter of 1914-15; bottom view is of approximately the same stretch of road following paving with concrete during winter of 1916-17.

## DANVILLE CHAMBER OF COMMERCE

The beginning of the Danville Chamber of Commerce goes back to 1889.

The 70 founding members of the Chamber of Commerce had a dream of a city thriving with industry and business. In 1900, they published a treatise setting forth clearly and truthfully the advantages of a city "whose financial and social conditions are on solid foundations; whose growth has been steady and substantial, and whose environments are such that it must always grow."

The first chamber officers were as follows: President, Gus M. Greenebaum; first vice president, W.E. Shedd; second vice president, Charles H. Hecht; secretary, F.O. French, and C.L. English, treasurer.

In 1916, the Danville Chamber of Commerce came of age and joined the then-growing chamber movement in firming its goals and purposes for community betterment. Part of that decision made by the chamber's board of directors was to put the management of the organization, under the board's direction, in the hands of a person specially trained to do this job on a full-time basis. Peter L. Willis was the first manager to serve, remaining until 1919, when he was succeeded by Allen T. Gordon.

One of the earliest location for the chamber's offices was at 6 E. Main Street, now a part of the parking lot of Towne Centre.
Taken from a story by Jane Mauck

## DOWNTOWN DANVILLE

Downtown Danville's skyline changed dramatically in the 25 years between 1895 and 1920.

The first of these changes came in 1896 with the completion of the Daniel Building, a four-story structure of red sandstone, featuring a tower-like corner surmounted by a tall turret. It housed professional offices on the upper floors with the F.W. Woolworth Company 5-and-10-cent store occupying the ground level and basement for many years. The building was--and is--on the northwest corner of the public square.

In 1901, a six-story building was erected one block north, on the northwest corner of Vermilion and North streets. It was named the Temple Building because Masonic lodges occupied the top floor. The first and second floors and basement were leased for 20 years to the Emery Dry Goods Company; the balance of the building was devoted to professional offices. Dr. George McCann, a leading dentist who had captained the Northwestern University's football team in his youth, had his office here.

On the other side of Vermilion Street, a five-story structure which became known as the Adams Building was erected in 1906. The Inter-State Water Company offices were located on the ground floor for many years while the upper stories were occupied by lawyers and doctors.

On the east side of Vermilion Street's unit block, the Baum Building was erected in 1907. An elevator lobby on the ground floor provided access to professional offices on the floors above. At various times over the years, the basement housed such diverse tenants as a barber shop and headquarters of the local chapter of the American Cancer Society.

HEAVIEST LOAD

A teamster sits atop an 18-ton stone slab while patient horses await the order to move out. Danville Transfer & Storage Company had the drayage contract for moving building materials to the site of the new federal building and post office between 1909 and 1911. This picture was taken August 1, 1910. The man wearing a white shirt, straw hat and smoking a pipe, is Carey B. Hall, owner of the transfer firm. As a younger man, he had a brief, disastrous career as a streetcar motorman. He was unable to stop his car at the end of the track on Fairchild Street at Logan Avenue and the car rolled down Waterworks Hill.

## SHORT-LIVED FACILITY

Indicative of Danville's rapid growth, this imposing post office building, erected in 1893, was vacated in 1911, when the new post office and federal court building across N. Vermilion Street in the 200 block was ready for occupancy. Later, the building housed offices of the Danville Chamber of Commerce. The building at left became the Carlton Hotel (after its owner Carl Trough) and it, too, was razed many years ago.

## THE WAY IT WAS

The mansion of Mike Kelly, millionaire coal baron, occupied the entire block between Madison Street on the left and Harrison Street, fronting on Vermilion Street. The new Danville Carnegie Library, opened in 1904, is at left in photograph. Note the horse and buggy on Harrison Street, the double line of streetcar tracks on Vermilion and the brick pavement. The Kelly home was torn down in 1909 to make way for a new federal courthouse and post office, which opened in midsummer, 1911.

After the new federal building was opened for business in midsummer of 1911, Danville's Gov. Bradford Chapter, Daughters of the American Revolution, decided it needed a touch of class—and made sure that it got one. This photograph, taken some years later, shows the memorial to Revolutionary War soldiers buried in Vermilion County (their names are inscribed in the sidewalk at the base). A replica of Daniel French's famed sculpture, "The Minute Man," tops the shaft rising from the pedestal base.

Occupied in mid-summer of 1911, the handsome U.S. Courthouse and Post Office, situated on the site of the old Mike Kelly mansion between Madison and Harrison Streets on Vermilion, was the pride of the year. The post office used the first floor; second and third floors contained other federal offices and a courtroom. Construction began in September, 1909, and was a heavy labor project, involving the moving of massive slabs of Bedford stone.

A TOUCH OF CLASS

PRIDE OF 1911

## MAN WHO MADE HIS MARK

John Beard was only 69 when he died in 1921 but he had left a lasting imprint on Danville. As proprietor of an ice company, he built a dam on the North Fork River near Ellsworth Park and harvested the ice, later changing the business to artificial ice-making, distributing the product through the city by fleets of horse-drawn ice wagons and later trucks; as a contractor, he was first to pave the city's streets and he built the first City Hall in 1896; as a stone mason, he designed and built the stone arch bridge on Main Street over Stony Creek, considered a masterpiece of engineering and masonry; as a politician, he was mayor of Danville three times; as a newspaper publisher, he owned the Danville Press.

## MAN OF MANY PARTS

William Ray Jewell, a native Hoosier, had enough careers for several men. He was a Civil War officer, a Christian church minister, the publisher of the Danville *Daily News* (consolidated with the Danville *Daily Commerical* in 1903) and postmaster of Danville for 24 years under five presidents: Arthur, Benjamin Harrison, William McKinley, Theodore Roosevelt and William Howard Taft.

## JOURNALIST-SCHOLAR

Clint C. Tilton was editor of the Danville *Press-Democrat*, which became the Morning Press under his ownership prior to its ultimate sale to the *Commercial-News* in 1927. Tilton was one of Illinois' leading Lincoln scholars and was a technical adviser for the motion picture, *Abe Lincoln in Illinois*.

## PRESS GENIUS

William J. Parrett was the financial member of the Harrison-Parrett team that took the *Commercial-News* from 900 daily circulation in 1897 to 30,000 in 1930. Parrett originated the Dollar Day sales promotion plan nationally, was responsible for establishing the first municipal golf course in Illinois in Ellsworth Park, inspired the idea of combined charities which resulted in today's United Way organization. He became publisher on Harrison's death in 1930, died three years later.

## PHILANTHROPIST-PUBLISHER

John Higgins Harrison came to Danville in 1897 and bought a part interest in the *Evening Commercial,* a struggling newspaper with 900 daily circulation. He succeeded in obtaining a merger with the rival *Morning News* in 1903, eventually became majority stockholder. Together with his financially-astute partner, William J. Parrett, he increased circulation to 30,000 daily by the time of his death in 1930. As recounted elsewhere, he had a great altruistic interest in his adopted city, one that lives on today in one of Danville's finest recreation areas, Harrison Park. He also contributed a large sum of money to his alma mater, DePauw University in Greencastle, Indiana for the construction of a building which was named in his honor.

## PASTURE NEXT STOP

These were the last horse-drawn fire wagons in Danville. The picture at the top was in front of the Germantown Fire Station, which had served as the municipal building for Germantown, an incorporated village in the early years of the century before its annexation to Danville. The wagon in the bottom picture was in front of Station Number 3, Collett and Main Streets. The Stratman Blacksmith Shop was in the building at left. Both photographs were taken in 1911.

Two Danville firemen were killed in this spectacular 1915 blaze which virtually destroyed the IOOF Building at 125 N. Vermilion Street. Woodbury Book Company, which occupied the ground floor was badly damaged but a portrait of Christ was recovered amidst the rubble untouched by flames. The firemen lost their lives when a wall collapsed. The photographer might have caught the split-second aftermath of the tragedy; note the ladder in the act of falling.

## TRAGIC FIRE

## SPECTACULAR FIRE

This spectacular fire on March 15, 1898, brought a large crowd to the unit block of N. Vermilion Street. Firemen play streams of water on the Golden Rule Department Store, virtually obscured by flames and smoke. The building to the left in picture seems untouched by the blaze. Golden Rule stood on the site later occupied by the S.S. Kresge Company store on the alley. The store suffered two other major fires, one in 1915 and a second in the early 1920s, the latter forcing it out of business.

## SPEEDY STEED

When Fire Chief Perry Cessna wanted to get to a fire in a hurry in 1911, he had a swift horse to pull his fast-rolling, rubber-tired rig. The big bell on front was operated by a foot pedal; its clangor, accompanied by the sound of galloping hooves, promptly cleared the way. Photograh was taken in front of Engine House No. 1, built in 1890, next to the old City Hall The site is now covered by the municipal parking garage.

## 'HOT' COMBINATION

This rubber-tired fire wagon and spirited team of horses made a "hot" combination to fight fires in Danville at the turn of the century. An unidentified fireman holds the reins of the wagon in front of Station No. 2, built in 1898 and located just north of the railroad tracks on N. Walnut Street.

## PROUD FIREFIGHTER

Ira Cronkhite is the driver of this first motorized unit, an American-LaFrance combination hose and chemical truck. The time was 1911 and location was the Madison Square Fire Station, now housing a retail business. The fire department was completely motorized in 1919.

## THE CROWDS GATHER

Back in the summer of 1913, it was the same as it is today. Whenever a fire breaks out and firemen rush to the scene, the crowds gather. This fire badly damaged the building housing Illinois Printing Company, corner of North and N. Vermilion streets. When the ashes cooled, the structure had to be virtually rebuilt. But the printing firm did not return. Instead, it relocated in a new building at the corner of North and Walnut streets, one block west, where it remained for more than 50 years. The 113-year-old business now is located on W. Williams Street.

# DANVILLE JUNCTION

To veteran railroad travelers in the late 19th and early 20th centuries, Danville Junction was a name synonymous with a hustle and bustle of activity.

For the casual passersby, the Junction was such a busy place that some found it difficult to believe that it was not in the heart of the city.

Trains chugged into and out of the station regularly. Passengers walked back and forth between nearby business establishments and the station. Express and baggage wagons were wheeled hither and yon. Drivers of horse-drawn cabs waited nearby for a paying fare.

The Junction was used by five railroads for their passenger travel and baggage and express business. Activity there was large enough to support a number of businesses, including restaurants, four hotels, newsstand, barber shop, drug store and saloons.

It was here that travelers waited for connections to other railroads or grabbed a bite to eat while their train was readied for transfer between the lines' various divisions.

The Junction was formed by the intersection of the Wabash Railroad and what became the Peoria & Eastern Railroad, in 1869. Their juncture near Williams Street, with Collett Street on the east, formed a small wedge-shaped area.

Junction station was owned by Hiram Beckwith who leased the building to the Wabash. Beckwith also was the owner of the adjoining Annex Hotel.

The station included a ticket office, lunch room and separate waiting rooms for men and women.

In addition to the stop at the Junction, railroads also had stations closer to the main part of town. The Chicago & Eastern Illinois (C&EI) had its North Street Station while the Peoria & Eastern predecessor (the Big Four) had facilities on Gilbert and later on Vermilion Street. The Wabash had its station on E. Main Street.

But in its heyday, the Junction had more activity than any of the other stations. Almost everyone traveling in the Midwest passed through.

It was here that Presidents McKinley and Roosevelt greeted crowds of well-wishers in 1899 and 1904 respectively.

The Junction enjoyed a rapid growth and a relatively short period of importance. Its decline into oblivion occurred just as quickly.

A number of circumstances were responsible.

One factor was the construction of a new bridge into the city from the west on the Big Four's Cairo Division. The Junction was by-passed on the new route which resulted.

The C&EI Shops were moved from near the Junction to Oaklawn in 1904. The transfer meant a loss of business created by C&EI officials and workers who used the Junction as a center for downstate activities.

In the same year, the Wabash erected a new depot on its downtown site and the road's better trains discontinued stops at the Junction.

Then in 1916 and 1917, the C&EI built a handsome passenger station on Fairchild Street, above the recently completed (1915) vehicular traffic subway.

Growth of interurban business, centered downtown, was another factor.

The change in the nation's transportation habits brought on by the automobile was the final blow.

Danville Junction and businesses around it struggled on for a few years. The station was closed, reopened, and closed for good in 1919. Only memories remain.

## A SLOW DAY?

Arrival of the Big Four passenger train from Peoria seems to find few Indianapolis-bound customers waiting at the depot on N. Vermilion Street. This photograph was taken sometime between 1900 and 1905. Note the horse-drawn U.S. Mail wagon waiting at the east end of the passenger station.

'A GOOD CIGAR'S A SMOKE!'

Back in the male chauvinist days before World War I, a tag of a whimsical verse concluded: "A woman's only a woman/But a good cigar's a smoke!" Cigars were a man's preference and most cities of Danville's size could boast one or more cigar factories. Klein's Cigar Factory at 521-523 E. Main Street turned out its leader brand, "Big Dick." In this 1910 photograph employees take a break to pose for the cameraman. A skilled cigarmaker could hand roll as many as 250 cigars a day. Retail prices in cigar stores ranged from a nickel to 15 cents on the average.

The Mill Street Bridge connected the major area of the city with Vermilion Heights from Logan Avenue, spanning the North Fork River at the north end of Ellsworth Park. Historians are silent as to the means of access prior to 1915 when this bridge was built; where a predecessor span was located is unclear. Mill Street Bridge also carried State Route 1 west until Dan Beckwith Bridge on W. Main Street was built in 1948. The structure pictured still stands but is crumbling and has been closed even to pedestrians for several decades.

BRIDGE TO THE HEIGHTS

105

## WHY ALL DOLLED UP?

Why Ross C. Kiningham's team and delivery wagon were decorated in this photograph is unclear but obviously the piano and organ dealer, standing beside the wagon, was proud of their appearance, possibly as the tail-end of a street parade. Even the date of the picture is obscure, inasmuch as the figure, "about 1915," accompanying it is clearly incorrect. The photographer took the picture no later than 1909; construction began then on the present federal courthouse (until recently also the post office) behind the wagon at right. And it had to be taken prior to 1914, the year the old YMCA building was erected behind Danville Public Library on the left. Note bricks with which W. Madison Street was paved.

## MAIN STREET MAINSTAY

Thomas Conron Hardware Company, wholesale and retail hardware and sporting goods, was a mainstay of E. Main Street at 116-120, for many years. It used most of the space in the big two-story building except for the comparatively small area leased to the Boston Store. Its neighbor to the west across the alley was the Meis Bros. Department Store, founded in 1897 by Alphonse and Joseph Meis, immigrants from Alsace-Lorraine, and a retail business leader for more than 60 years. The Conron business survives today in its wholesale aspect as Conron, Inc.

## SOURCE OF ENERGY

This 1916 photo of the interior of the Danville Street Railway and Light Company shows the main generator that provided the city with electricity and powered the streetcar lines. Excess of the steam that drove the generators was sold to heat businesses and residences in the downtown and near-downtown areas. "City heat" was popular for many years.

Illinois Power Company powerhouse had only one smokestack after 1914 but it was a whopper, towering 250 feet into the sky, making it the highest structure in Danville. After construction of the Vermilion Power Station near Oakwood, power generation for Danville was transferred there. The big smokestack was razed in June, 1967.

## HIGHEST POINT

Building a pumping station in 1912 was a big step forward for Inter-State Water Company, which had begun operations in 1883 as a supplier of water to the city of Danville for the purpose of fighting fires. At that time, water was pumped directly from the North Fork River and there were no private customers. But after building a water treatment plant in 1902, business increased dramatically in terms of domestic consumers.

## BIG STEP FORWARD

## BIGGEST ANYWHERE

If there had been a Guinness Book of World Records then, Danville's Western Brick Company would have been listed as the largest brickyard in the world. With a main plant and two subsidiary yards, the company more than tripled its 1901 production of 30 million brick to 100 million in 1916. Western's brick built the Conrad Stevens Hotel in Chicago, the world's largest, Memorial Stadium in Champaign and most of the University of Illinois campus buildings. In later years, the beehive kilns gave way to a computerized tunnel kiln that provided quality control of heat and material and speeded production.

## PROVIDING THE COMPETITION

Western Brick Company was the giant among local brickyards but the Danville Brick Company, located in Vermilion Heights, provided competition in the first two decades of the 20th century. The photograph is dated "about 1920" but the cars pictured appear to be of 1915-18 vintage.

## TWIN INDUSTRIES

This 1915 artist's sketch depicts Allith Prouty Company, hardware manufacturers, and the allied firm, Danville Malleable Iron Company. Allith Prouty which began operations in 1912 existed for more than 50 years and played an important role in packaging production during World War II.

## STURDY SURVIVOR

This 1916 photograph is of the Danville Country Club's clubhouse. In 1927, the country club bought land west of Lake Vermilion, built a clubhouse and an 18-hole golf course. John Harrison, principal owner of the *Commercial-News,* subsequently bought the former property, including the 9-hole golf course and woods on both sides of the North Fork River and gave it to the city as a public park in memory of his mother. Today, 71 years later, Harrison Park Clubhouse looks much the same.

# DANVILLE COURTHOUSE

The story of how Danville got a new courthouse back in 1912 should rank high in any saga of American political skulduggery.

It's the type of tale sure to make any Chicago alderman shake his head in admiring wonder and mutter to himself, "I wish I could think up something like that!"

The Vermilion County courthouse, built in 1876, was a handsome structure and served admirably for a few years. But Danville and the county were growing so fast that by the turn of the century it became apparent that a larger hall of justice was needed desperately.

There was just one catch: Money.

The county didn't have it. And the board of supervisors had the depressing conviction that a bond issue referendum would be resoundingly defeated by tax-sensitive citizens. Worse, the public might be so incensed that some board members could be out of work, come the next election.

What to do?

Some ingenious soul came up with a suggestion that would have endeared him to the late Chicago Mayor Richard Daley in a similar situation.

We can't get building funds by raising taxes, he said, stating the obvious. And we haven't a prayer of getting money through a bond issue referendum.

But we can raise taxes to repair and remodel the courthouse, he declared happily. And lawyers who liked the idea agreed that his suggestion was entirely legal.

So the die was cast.

First, the old cornerstone was removed and replaced at the rear of the building.

This was the remodeling.

Next, the courthouse was torn down to the ground. Then it was rebuilt, bigger, roomier, more attractive.

This was the repair.

Whether the public was hoodwinked by the high jinks, whether the board members who acquiesced in the legal scam were able to hold their jobs, is a matter in the mists of the past 75 years.

But the fact is that the "remodeled and repaired" courthouse has served adequately for a long time. And by the mid-1980s county government was able to make use of the gift of the old Daniel Building across the street and build an annex for many county offices.

As they often say in Cook County, "Where there's a will (and a few good schemers around) there's a way."

## TAKING SHAPE

In this 1912 photograph looking north on Vermilion Street it is evident that the "remodeled" (read new) Vermilion County Courthouse is rapidly taking shape. Note advertising on board fence surrounding the construction site.

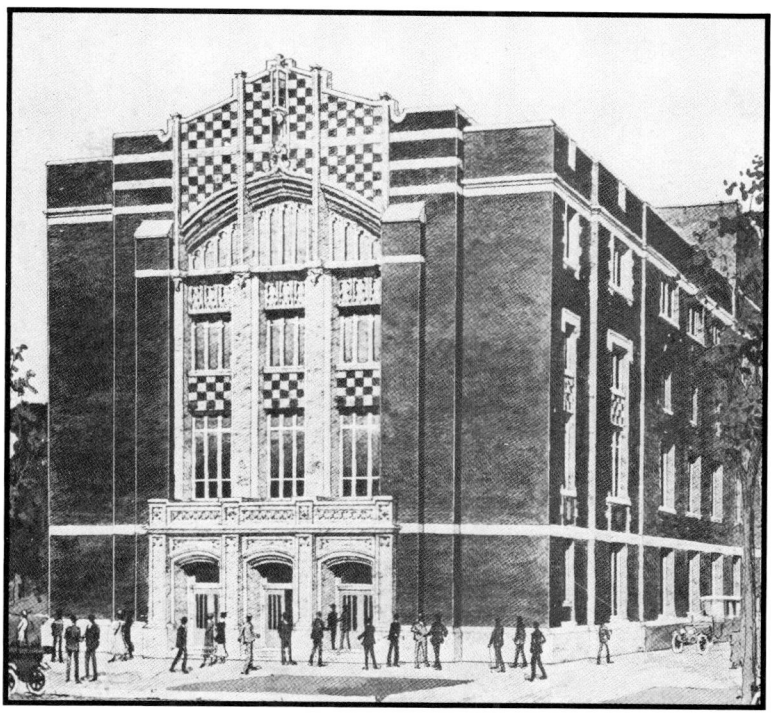

## IMPROVING LIFE

Three buildings not absolutely essential to preserving life but definitely intended to improve the quality of life were erected in Danville in the decade beginning in 1910.

The first of these was the Elks Club (below), a handsome three-story brick building, erected in 1914 across the alley to the north from the Danville Public Library. It housed Lodge 332, Benevolent & Protective Order of Elks, had billiards and game rooms and on the third floor several sleeping rooms which were rented out to bachelor members of the order. The lower level, which came to be known as the Elks Corral, housed a restaurant. The second floor was used for lodge meetings and doubled as a ballroom for dancing.

After the lodge and club built the Elks Country Club on E. Liberty Lane in the 1960s, the downtown building became the property of the Danville Recreation Department. Ultimately it was sold and the building razed. The site is now a used car sales lot.

The second building was the Young Men's Christian Association (top left), erected in 1915 behind Danville Public Library, with entrances on W. Madison and N. Hazel streets. It had a swimming pool, bowling alley, weightlifting room and steam baths. The upper floors contained rooms rented to young men for a nominal fee.

It was razed after the new Family YMCA was built on N. Vermilion Street in the 1960s. The site is now a parking lot for library patrons.

The final building of the three, the Masonic Temple (top right) on W. North Street, was dedicated in 1917. It took the place of the temple on the top floor of the Temple Building and housed headquarters of subordinate lodges and both Scottish and York Rite orders. It has a fine auditorium and stage, a dining room and complete facilities for rituals of the order.

The motorcycle was only 26 years old (it was invented by Gottlieb Daimler, a German) when this 1911 picture was taken. But these Excelsior models look surprisingly modern. Riders are W.I. "Pop" Bowman, left, then 22 years old, and Earl Gillis. Bowman became Danville's most famous photographer-historian and Gillis, for many years, was employed by American Railway Express Company.

TEMPLINE OF FINANCE

The Ionic columns that grace the front of the Second National Bank, 27 N. Vermilion Street, were typical of the classic look favored by architects for bank design in the early part of the 20th century. The picture was taken in 1916. Note signs of lawyers' offices in second floor windows: Curtis G. Redden and C.H. Beckwith.

It was 1916 and Trent Brothers Lumber and Planing Mill at 522 Franklin Street was proud of its new hard-rubber tired truck. But the firm still depended on old-fashioned horsepower to move its wares as the above photograph proves.

DOBBIN STILL POPULAR

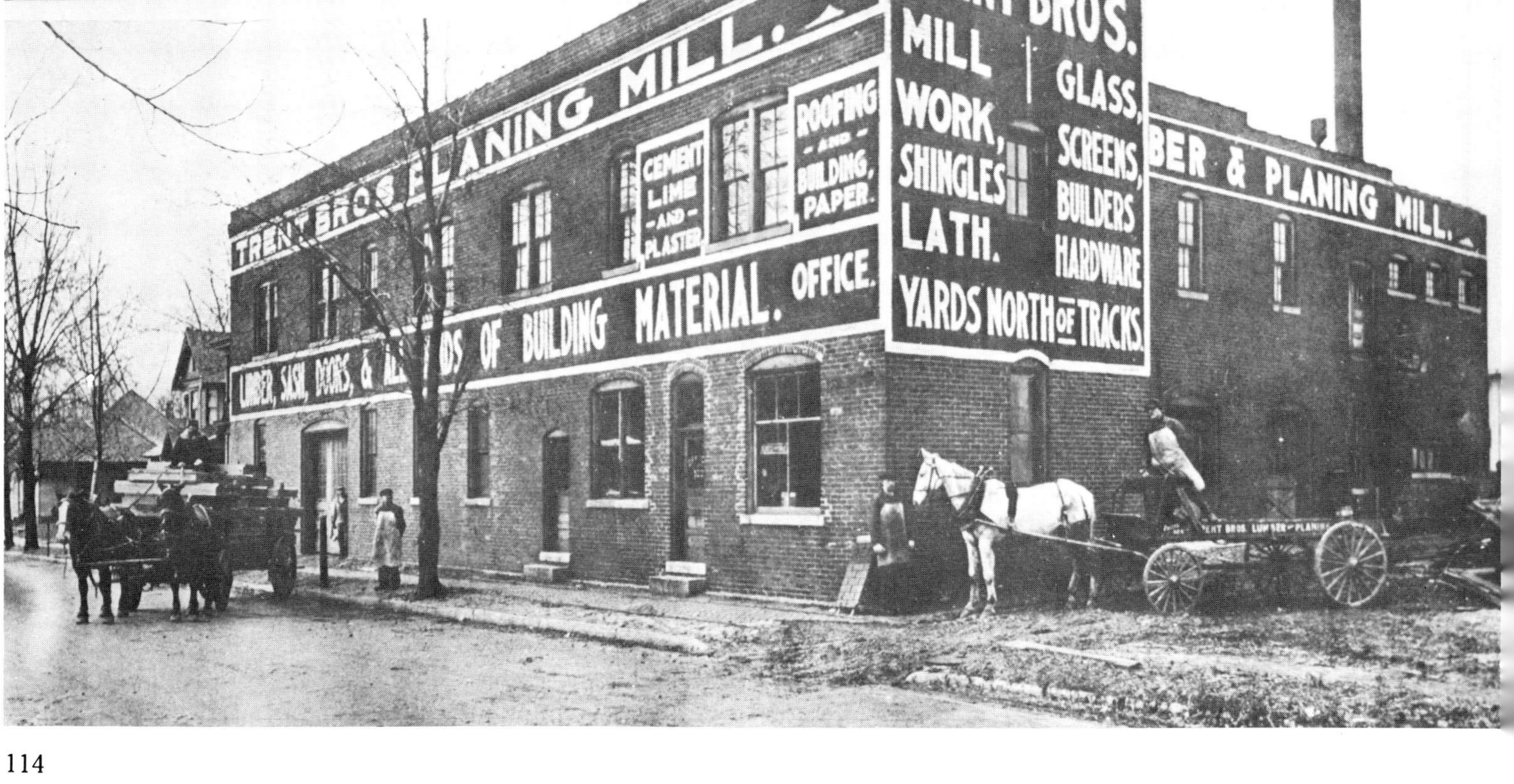

## TEDDY CAMPAIGNS

The year was 1912—probably in the fall—and Teddy Roosevelt was in Danville campaigning for president on the Bull Moose ticket. The bunting-draped stand was in the southeast corner of the public square, Conspicuously absent from among the notables on the stand was "Uncle Joe" Cannon, who would have nothing to do with T.R. when the former president split from the regular GOP to seek a third party bid. Roosevelt outpolled Republican President William Howard Taft but lost to Democrat Woodrow Wilson in the November election.

When east side shoppers went to the William Stuebe Grocery Store 79 years ago, they expected to buy only groceries. If they wanted meat, they went next door on E. Main Street to Kuemmerle's Meat Market. Stuebe's son, Albert, awaits customers in this picture taken May 9, 1908. *Photo courtesy of Harriet Pashe*

## BEFORE SUPERMARKETS

115

## WORLD WAR I HERO

Curtis G. Redden was a native of Rossville, Illinois, but after graduating from the University of Michigan where he was a football star, he opened a law office in Danville. He saw service in the Spanish-American War, commanded Battery A as a captain, was promoted to battalion commander as a major and at the end of World War I, he was a lieutenant colonel and commander of the 149th Field Artillery Regiment. He died of pneumonia in 1919 in Coblenz, Germany, and is buried in Danville's Spring Hill Cemetery. Danville's public square is named for him in addition to a street and an American Legion post.

## FIRST AIRMAN TO DIE

William Jewell Whyte, 21, was the first aviator from Danville to lose his life in World War I—on March 20, 1918, "somewhere in France." Whyte, who played football at the University of Chicago after graduating from Danville High School, left the city on April 1, 1917, five days before the United States declared war against Germany. He was aboard ship en route to France when Congress approved President Wilson's action. He served six months as a volunteer ambulance driver for the French army, coming under fire many times. He then enlisted in the aviation branch of the U.S Signal Corps and had been commissioned a first lieutenant only a few days before his fatal crash. This city's Veterans of Foreign Wars Post 728 is named in his honor. Margaret Bradfield, a Danville native and cousin of the World War I hero, made the above sketch.

## THEY DIDN'T RETURN

Charles Bradley, above left, and Wayman "Hickey" Maberry, right, members of Danville's Company L, 8th Illinois Infantry, died in France in World War I. Maberry was killed by a German sniper. The manner of Bradley's death is unknown; he was missing in action but his body later was recovered. They were lost in the autumn of 1918 during the great Allied Meuse-Argonne offensive that broke the back of German resistance. Chartered in 1919, American Legion Post 736 honored these heroes with their names. Both men are buried in Soldiers Circle Springhill Cemetery.

# WORLD WAR I

All three Danville National Guard outfits were called into federal service in the first World War and all went overseas. A fourth, Company B, 3rd Illinois Infantry, from Hoopeston also served in France.

Company B and Danville's Battery A and Company L were accustomed to federal service; the three outfits had been on the Mexican border for several months in 1916. The mobilization followed Mexican rebel leader Pancho Villa's attack on the U.S. border town of Columbus, N.M., earlier that year.

Company L was commanded by Capt. William Beeler, a local transfer and storage company proprietor, during his preview of war. But when the unit again was federalized, he failed to pass the physical examination. A Capt. William Crawford of the Regular Army was assigned as commanding officer when the company reached Ft. Sam Houston, Tex. Other Danville officers were 1st Lt. Frank Robinson (a long inactive Veterans of Foreign Wars post was named in his honor) and 2nd Lt. Floyd Chavis. Both these men returned home safely.

The company, consisting entirely of black soldiers, participated in some of the heaviest fighting. According to Jack M. Williams' "History of Vermilion County," 49 died in action, including Charles Bradley and Wayman "Hickey" Maberry, for whom the Bradley-Maberry American Legion Post 736 is named. The 132 volunteers who left Danville were recruited to a strength of 197 at the training camp.

Company I, which became Company D, lost only one member of the original roster in action: Cpl. Olen Fultz, Capt. A.C. Reynolds and Sgt. Mathias "Si" Swindall were wounded. This, despite being in combat in the Amiens and Verdun sectors and in the Meuse-Argonne offensive.

Company B was in the Albert sector and also Meuse-Argonne.

Battery A first saw action at St. Mihiel, the first "all American" engagement of the war and was credited with firing the first shot in the bombardment of German positions. Like the other units it was on occupation duty after the Armistice. It was during this period that its beloved former commander, Lt. Col. Curtis G. Redden (who recently had been promoted to executive officer of the 149th Field Artillery Regiment) died of pneumonia in Coblenz, Germany. He was 37 years old.

---

## THE BOYS COME HOME

Not only Johnny came marching home on May 10, 1919, but Jimmy and Joe, Billy and Bob. As battle-tested members of Battery A turn north on Vermilion at E. Main Street, they cross the square which now perpetuates the name of the man who led them to war but did not return—then Capt. Curtis G. Redden. The man leading the unit is Capt. William W. Bodine of Villanova, Pennsylvania, who died in 1961. He succeeded Redden when the latter became executive officer of the 149th Field Artillery.

## TEACHER AND HER PUPILS

Jessie Said, who taught cooking at Danville High School, poses with some of her pupils in this photograph taken March 2, 1896. From left, Olive Duke, Miss Said, Margaret Parle, Allie Lewis, Helen Deutsch and Reva J. Seed. Miss Said became the wife of Dr. Herschel Baldwin, prominent Danville ophthalmologist.

## WAS SCHOOL OUT?

The occasion for this 1906 photograph of Fairchild School teachers is not indicated but from the attire and foliage of trees in the background it very well could have been in observance of the last day of school before the start of the long summer vacation.

## HAPPY B FIFTH!

These youngsters in Grade B5 at Franklin School dressed up for this special picture, probably signifying the last day before the start of summer vacation, 1906. The blonde girl in the white dress, seated in the second row, was Ruth Schecter, mother of Nancy Voss of Danville. *Photo courtesy of Nancy Voss*

## PRIZED MEMENTO

A prized memento of Clarence Ost, 505 Wilkin Road, is this 1908 picture of the old Fairchild School's room IV pupils. Ost, a retired employee of the Danville Post Office, is sixth from left in the front row.

## A TIME OF TRANSITION

Although this photograph of the 600 block of N. Vermilion Street is not dated, the vintage of automobile and truck pictured suggests 1912. That this was a time of transition is indicated not only by the motor vehicles but also by the streetcar tracks and the presence of hitching posts along the curb.

Built before 1916, the Palmer National Bank was occupying the southeast corner of the public square in this 1925 picture. A bigger building replaced it on the site. Now, directly opposite, across Towne Centre, stands the modernistic-styled Palmer-American National Bank on what would have been the southwest corner of the square. The American in the name is the result of a 1931 merger with the American Bank and Trust Company. That bank, established in 1907, was located at 112 E. Main Street.

'ANCHOR' BANK

# TALL TOWER

This photograph of the First National Bank Building must have been taken shortly after completion of the two-year building project in 1918, judging from the vacant look of windows above the second floor. At 12 stories, this was Danville's own "skyscraper"; the bank occupied the first floor, mezzanine and lower level. Upper floors soon were occupied by offices of doctors, dentists, lawyers, stock brokers and loan companies. The Savoy Hotel is at left, the Daniel Building at right. The present name of the big building is Bresee Tower, after the Champaign, Illinois family which presently owns it.

## BREWING A BETTER BEER

Fecker Brewing Company beer was popular in Danville, where it was brewed in this complex of buildings, and throughout the Midwest back around the turn of the century. During Prohibition the company turned to making a near-beer with indifferent success. When Repeal came in the early 1930s, the brewing of beer was resumed but the company found that it could not compete profitably with the giants of the industry. The buildings were sold to the Lauhoff Grain Company of Chicago in the early 1940s and a Danville milling operation was begun. The company expanded tremendously, manufacturing a variety of corn and soybean based products. It is now a wholly-owned subsidiary of Bunge, Inc.

## MODEST-PRICED HOSTELRY

Built around the turn of the century, the Savoy Hotel at 8 W. Main Street catered mainly to the budget-minded trade. This picture, taken around 1915, shows the First National Bank building at right. Note the fancy five-globe streetlights at the curb, much more elegant than anything in recent years. The Savoy later was purchased by a national hotel chain and renamed the Milner. It was destroyed by fire in 1954. The Courthouse Annex, which wraps around Bresee Tower from Vermilion Street, now occupies the site.

## CARING FOR CHILDREN

This was the scene in August, 1916, at the Children's Home, located on the corner of Logan Avenue and Williams Street. Orphans and children from broken homes who had become wards of the court were sheltered there for indefinite periods of time. Later, two brick buildings were put up to serve the needs of the children better. Over the years, the home has altered its mission to cope with changing societal conditions and has received state funds.

The Plaza Hotel, pictured here in 1913, was regarded by many travelers as the best in Illinois outside Chicago. The structure first saw life in 1859 as Lincoln Hall, built by Dr. W.W.R. Woodbury, pioneer Danville doctor and pharmacist. When it became a hotel in the '90s, the front underwent a facelift to this more modern appearance. Woodbury Drug Company, founded in 1846, survives today as the Gulick Drug Company and the Danville National Bank merged with the Second National Bank around 1920. The building was razed as part of the urban renewal program of the 1960s and the Palmer-American Bank now stands on the site.

## DIGNIFIED ELEGANCE

The lobby of Danville's new Masonic Temple in 1920 reflected the prevailing mood of the times: An emphasis on dignified elegance. Furniture was heavy, even massive, with an accent on comfort. Note the silk fringe of the lampshades, the gilt frames of the pictures on the walls, and the beamed ceiling.

## FROM 'WASH HOUSE' TO YOUR HOUSE

The Billy Noll Sanitary Laundry, 120-124 N. Walnut Street, relieved Danville's housewives of the traditional Monday wash day blues by picking up laundry and delivering the washed product back to their doorsteps. Business must have been good, judging by the four covered delivery wagons. Although the photograph does not identify him, it's a fair guess that the gentleman behind the wheel of the automobile in the picture is proprietor Noll himself. The photograph is dated 1920 but the appearance of the car and the clothing worn by the women pictured suggest that the scene was snapped four or five years earlier.

## HISTORIAN

Lottie Jones, born in 1854, was the author of a comprehensive and highly-regarded *History of Vermilion County,* published in two volumes in 1911. She was one of the founders of Illinois Printing Company in 1874, a firm which is still in business in 1987. Miss Jones died in 1933.

## WOMEN IN THE WORKPLACE

This 1917 photograph of the interior of the Illinois Printing Company is indicative of the growing role of women in the workplace: Nine women are shown, equaling the number of men pictured. Note the man at right, obviously wearing a detachable collar on his shirt. *Photo courtesy of Ruby Burmeister*

FUN FOR THE FORCE

Shorty Lowe, the midget in the picture, worked for Ike Levin's Clothing Store at Main and Jackson. Levin thought it would be fun to dress him as a policeman. The hulking real-life Danville policemen were Joseph Reddy, left, and Bill Bracewell, the largest members of the force. This 1909 picture is courtesy of Robert Reddy, for many years a merchant policeman and the son of Joseph Reddy.

These were Danville's finest in 1907, even though the uniforms and helmets are the same as those made famous in the early silent film comedies. The officers in front with felt hats were, from left, Lou Spangler, chief; W.F. Stewart, turnkey (jailer); Johnson Gammel, desk sergeant, and John Donnelly, night captain. The setting is in front of the old City Hall on Walnut Street.

NOT KEYSTONE KOPS

## CHAPTER IV

## BOOM BUST AND BATTLE

1921 - 1950

Danville, like most other American cities, experienced major changes in the 30 years between 1920 and 1950.

With a population topping 30,000, it had moved out of the small town classification to that of small city. The Chamber of Commerce was exuberantly optimistic about the future. It encouraged the formation of the "One Hundred Thousand Club." Members attached a small plate above their automobile license plate bearing the slogan, "Danville—100,000 in the Making." Some residents were doubtful but most thought it was an attainable goal. And why not?

Five railroads served the city. Coal still was king in Vermilion County, agriculture brought more money into the economy than manufacturing (but manufacturing was gaining), mercantile trade was booming and Danville was a shipping center with connections to every part of the country.

Danville residents were proud of their new Lake Vermilion, which promised to be an inexhaustible reservoir for the Inter-State Water Company, serving the city. It also was a beautiful treat for travelers entering Danville from the north.

They also liked to show off to out-of-town guests their imposing new high school, built in 1923-24, at Fairchild and Jackson streets on what had been Williams' pasture and circus grounds. It cost a million dollars, a lot of money in those days.

Streetcars provided cheap, easily accessible transportation to every section of the city. Passenger train service was ideal; the Wabash was on the main line between St. Louis, Missouri, and Detroit, Michigan. The Peoria & Eastern (P&E), a division of the New York Central Railroad, linked the Illinois city with Indianapolis, Indiana. The Illinois Terminal Railroad provided quick and easy service to Vermilion County communities and to Champaign-Urbana, Springfield and St. Louis.

The Cairo division of the New York Central provided service to northern Indiana. The Chicago & Eastern Illinois Railroad (C&EI) gave superb service between Danville and Chicago; indeed, you also could travel all the way to Florida without changing trains by way of adjoining lines.

Inter-city and inter-state bus service grew in the 1920-1950 period. Illini-Swallow Lines linked Champaign-Urbana with Indianapolis via Danville while the Greyhound Lines connected Chicago, Danville and points south.

Danville's growth required new grade schools and the replacement of others. Cannon and Edison Schools were built in the 1920s and the original Lincoln and Fairchild Schools were replaced with new buildings in 1941.

A major political change occurred as well in the 1920s. Until 1927, the city was governed by a mayor and 10 aldermen (one each from 10 wards). But this was before civil service and municipal employees, including policemen and firemen were hired and fired on the basis of politics rather than merit. Citizens decided, in a special referendum, that the system was both inefficient and corrupt. They opted for the city commissioner form, which elected a mayor and four commissioners at-large. The mayor was ex-officio police commissioner; his colleagues presided over individual departments: Finance, public health and safety (including the fire and garbage departments), streets and public property (including the parks). The first mayor under the new system was Henry Hulce, a former buggy manufacturer.

Danville survived the Roaring Twenties rather well; there was no major crime attributed to the illicit liquor traffic. There were bootleggers aplenty and some even provided home delivery. One ingenious trick was to paint glass milk bottles white to hide the nature of the contents. To passersby, this appeared to look like a legitimate dairy business!

But the 1920s, which had started so well economically, did not end that way. Railroads were beginning to decline and that affected the mining industry. Many big underground mines closed. Smokestack factories were sharply curtailing production. Employees were laid off. The Chamber of Commerce, which only a few years earlier was optimistic, was now worried. Then someone came up with the brilliant Danville Plan, which proved so effective that many cities throughout the United States copied it.

In the plan, a not-for-profit corporation was formed, stock shares issued and investors bought shares. The money was used to build small factory structures. Factories elsewhere, looking for a better financial and industrial climate, were contacted and offered buildings on a cost basis price with long-term low interest mortgages plus a possible tax abatement for the first few years. As a result, several small factories moved to Danville. No single factory employed large numbers but the philosophy here was: "Better to have diversified industry than a one-industry town where a plant closing could bring heavy unemployment and dry up economic input." One such plant that benefitted both itself and Danville was the Fred W. Amend Company, creator of the famous "Chuckles" candy. Eventually, the firm became a subsidiary of Nabisco Corporation but recently was bought by private interests.

Danville was slow in being hit by the Great Depression. One of a number of reasons was the favorable effect on the economy of the Soldiers Home with its large federal payroll and the veterans spending their pension checks in the city. The function of the home, primarily domiciliary, changed in 1932 when the many agencies of the federal government concerned with veterans were consolidated into the Veterans Administration. As a result, the home underwent considerable remodeling and new construction including the million-dollar six-story Building 58, the hospital for the facility's new mission, the care and treatment of neuropsychiatric patients.

The low point of the Depression came in 1932 when 13 million were unemployed nationally out of a 39-million-member work force, or one out of three Americans without jobs. Some Danville observers figured the local ratio at about one out of four unemployed. When Franklin D. Roosevelt ordered a national bank moratorium in 1933 shortly after he was inaugurated, all three Danville banks closed. But all three, First National, Second National and Palmer-American, were so sound financially that they reopened on the first day the moratorium was lifted.

World War II was very much on Danville residents' minds long before Pearl Harbor; its two National Guard companies were federalized in 1940 and sent to Camp Forrest, Tennessee for training. Danville had approximately half of Vermilion County's 6,000 men and women in uniform. One hundred forty-five died in service; probably half of these casualties were from Danville. Outstanding heroes included Marine Maj. Kenneth Bailey, Congressional Medal of Honor (posthumously); Navy Cmdr. Joseph Taylor, Navy Cross; Army Air Forces Maj. W.R. Humrichouse, Silver Star, Distinguished Flying Cross; Army Capt. Robert Chapman, Silver Star.

The final years of the 1940 decade saw the establishment at Danville High School of a University of Illinois Extension Center, providing two years of college education. Soon it became Danville Junior College.

BIGGEST HOTEL

Built in 1926, the Hotel Wolford's nine-story bulk dominates this downtown scene, photographed in the 1950s. The Wolford had 250 transient rooms, and served as a community center where most service and civic organizations held regular luncheon or dinner meetings. The top floor was known as the "Sky Room." It was a large, mirrored ballroom, where many nationally-known big bands played for as many as 500 dancers. The Regency Room was an elegant dining room and the Vermilion Room was a sophisticated bar-lounge which sometimes featured strolling musicians. Today a remodeled Wolford provides efficiency apartments for elderly low income tenants on a rent-subsidized basis.

MEMORABLE EVENT

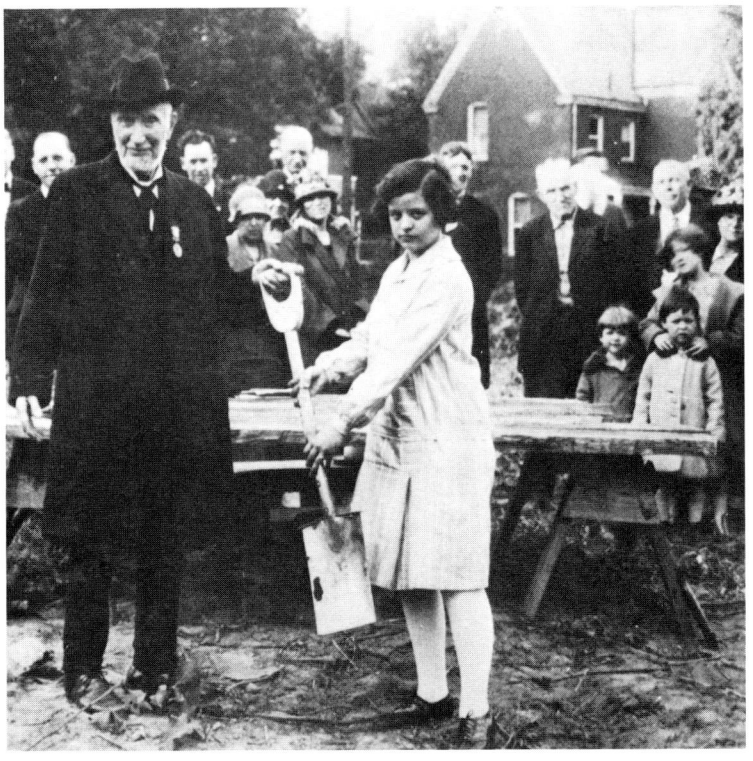

HONORING UNCLE JOE

This was the interesting scene in the Williams Street block between Vermilion and Walnut Streets in 1926. It was the groundbreaking for the St. James M.E. Church and the symbolic act was performed by Uncle Joe Cannon, retired from the House of Representatives, and the teen-age Ruth Burcham. The young girl grew up to become Ruth Howard, whose vocation was music but whose lifelong avocation was Danville history. Because of her personal contacts with many famous persons, her large collection of books and memorabilia, she was considered an outstanding authority on the city's past during her active years.

The Joseph G. Cannon School, built in 1925, honored Danville's most famous son. This photograph, taken the year of opening, illustrates the imposing front as seen by two generations of passersby on Main Street. The building is still in use as an elementary school.

# GREAT MOMENT IN HISTORY

In 1922, Danville's Uncle Joe Cannon, at right accepted an invitation to go to Washington, D.C., and take part in a momentous event--the dedication of the Lincoln Memorial. While there, he was caught in this candid camera shot with two other prominent Americans--President Warren G. Harding, left, and Robert Todd Lincoln, only surviving child of the Great Emancipator. It is obvious, comparing the height of Uncle Joe who was about five-foot-seven with Robert Lincoln, that the latter failed to inherit his father's height of six-foot-four.

Pallbearers from Curtis G. Redden Post 210, American Legion, wearing their World War I uniforms, gently place casket of Uncle Joe Cannon into the Berhalter Funeral Home hearse while a crowd of mourners gather round. The three ministers who shared in the service on November 13, 1926, are at right. The first is the Rev. Mr. Hindman of the First Presbyterian Church, then the Rev. Thomas Ewing of St. James Methodist (Uncle Joe's church) and finally, Father O'Riley of St. Patrick's Catholic Church. The scene is just north of the Cannon mansion at 418 N. Vermilion Street. Attending the funeral were Vice President Charles G. Dawes, U.S. Senator James Watson of Indiana, Illinois Governor Len Small and U.S. District Judge Walter C. Lindley. Uncle Joe is buried in Danville's Springhill Cemetery.

## SAYING GOODBYE TO UNCLE JOE

## CORNER OF THE PAST

This was the remodeled version of earlier structures but the legend at the top does not reflect the merger of the Palmer and American National Banks as do the signs at street level. This southeast corner of Redden Square was first occupied by a business structure in 1827 when Gurdon Hubbard built his frame Indian trading post there. Palmer now occupies its present imposing home directly west across from its former location. The 1940 photograph shows signs on S. Vermilion Street behind the bank; "Gymnasium" identifies the old Danville Gymnasium, long a training place for Golden Gloves boxers; "Terminal Lunch" had no morbid significance. It was so named because the Illinois Terminal Railroad (interurban) had its passenger station across the street in the north half of the Illinois Power Company building. All of area shown is now part of Towne Centre.

## ELEGANT INTERIOR

This was the ornate interior of the First National Bank when it was located in 12-story building which bore its name for more than 35 years, from 1918 to the early 1950s. It featured a great deal of marble and a story-and-a-half high ceiling. Note the fancy chandeliers and the wrought-iron face of the wall clock. The doors in the background opened into the elevator lobby and access to the upper 11 floors.

MONEY AND MUSIC

In this 1930 photograph, the accent was on money and music at the corner of Vermilion and Van Buren Streets. The principal structure was the Commercial Trust & Savings Bank, which consolidated with the First National Bank in 1931. The stairs inside the main entryway led up to the Kiningham Music Company, while the building immediately adjacent to the north, housed the Benjamin Temple of Music. The man standing outside that business is unidentified but might have been Horace Benjamin, a World War I veteran still living in 1987. Since the bank moved, the site has been occupied by numerous retail shops, including Betty Gay women's wear. The legend "Bank" remains on the building.

## A REAL SELF-MADE MAN

Tom Moses started working in coal mines as a youth and there met and became friends with another young man named John L. Lewis. Moses' wife, Robena, helped him expand his minimal education and, ever ambitious, he moved up the career ladder with ever-increasing-responsible jobs. He became superintendent of the big Bunsenville mine near Westville and later was president of U.S. Fuel Company. U.S. Fuel was a subsidiary of United States Steel. Near the end of his life, while residing in Danville, he was appointed director of the Illinois Department of Mines and Minerals. A son, Harry, duplicated his father's success and eventually became chief negotiator for mine operators in contract talks with the elder Moses' old friend, who also had reached the top as president of the United Mine Workers of America (UMWA).

## GREETING HIS FORMER BOSS

Danville's Jimmie Sloan, retired Secret Service agent and bodyguard of all the presidents from Teddy Roosevelt to Harry Truman, shakes hands with the man from Independence in this 1950 photograph.

## SPARKPLUG FOR DANVILLE

In the early days of his career as owner of a downtown shoe store, Frank P. Meyer posed for this 1921 photograph. He became interested in politics and in 1935 was elected Danville's second mayor under the commission form of government, a position he held until 1943. His two sons, Francis J. "Bus" and John P., shared their father's enthusiasm for politics. Both served as circuit judges and "Bus" also was county judge. John served in both the Illinois House of Representatives and the Illinois Senate. Both served with distinction in World War II; "Bus" as a lieutenant-commander in the Navy and John as a captain in Patton's Third Army in Europe. Their father was such a non-stop salesman of Danville while mayor that his fellow city executives elected him president of the Illinois Municipal League.

## RECALLING THE OLD DAYS

In 1926, the *Commercial-News* observed its 60th anniversary by giving itself a facelift. Improvements included a new stone front, waist-high counters of marble enclosing business office, classified advertising, retail advertising and circulation areas on the first floor, enlarged newsroom upstairs and a new larger rotary press in the basement. During several days of open house, visitors observed a printer at work, John Conley, who demonstrated how he set type by hand when the *Commercial* opened for business the year after the Civil War ended. The shallow, compartmented box in front of him contained the individual type faces. The top half contained capital letters, the bottom half the common letters. Proofreaders came to mark on galley proofs "u.c." or upper case when a capital letter should have been used or "l.c." or lower case when a common letter was needed.

## TALENT IN THE RAW

That this gawky 18-year-old kid would be inducted into baseball's Hall of Fame some day probably would have been roundly derided by his Danville Veterans teammates back in 1923. But the kid, who was trying out for a position on the Three-I League team was Red Ruffing, who became one of the New York Yankees immortals with his pitching talent. And, yes, he did become a member of the Hall of Fame.

# IMPROVING WITH AGE

Danville Country Club was built in 1927 but as this 1960 photograph indicates, it doesn't get older, it gets better. The watered fairways and lovingly-cared-for greens make the 18-hole course one of the finest in the Midwest. The clubhouse is the building near the center of the picture, with the swimming pool to its left. The smaller building at the right is the pro shop. Lake Vermilion is in the background and the winding drive leads to Denmark Road, thence to Danville.

Built in 1917, this grandstand was the focal point of the Illinois & Indiana (I&I) Fair, situated where the Fair Oaks Housing Authority project is located today. This 1925 photograph is devoid of people but on a day or night of harness racing it was packed to overflowing. After the I&I fair went out of business, the Eastern Illinois Fair held its annual exposition here and on adjacent ground.

## WHEN HARNESS RACING WAS KING

## CELEBRITY IN TOWN

The Danville Veterans of the Three-I League (Iowa, Illinois and Indiana) opened its 1923 season at its spacious Soldiers Home park in style. Kenesaw Mountain Landis, baseball's first commissioner, was in town and threw out the ceremonial first ball. Sharing the limelight with him were, far left, A.R. Samuel, president of the Second National Bank, and, far right, U.S. District Judge Walter C. Lindley.

## FOR THE BOYS OF SUMMER

One of the most-needed facilities for Danville after World War II was the Danville Stadium at Ninth Street. This photograph was taken about 1948. The stadium has been home to several minor league teams, most of them major league farm clubs. First of these was the Danville Dodgers, sponsored by the Brooklyn Dodgers, in the Three-I (or Three-Eye) League. That team won the pennant in 1946, largely because of the pitching of Carl Erskine, who went on to star for the parent Dodgers. The field itself is named the Wischer-Roose Field, honoring the late Rubie Wischer and Frank Roose, men who devoted a great deal of time, talent, energy and money to the preservation and encouragement of baseball in Danville.

## ELEGANT EDIFICE

For many years, the First Methodist Church, later St. James, was a Danville showplace, with its imposing tower, stained glass windows and ornate architecture. But by 1920, when this picture was taken, a growing congregation dictated a larger home. So land was purchased catercornered across the intersection on the northwest corner of Vermilion and Williams Streets for a new church home.

## LAST PRIOR TO WAR

Built in 1941 at 901 W. Fairchild Street, the Bethel Lutheran Church was the last structure of any size or importance built before the United States was drawn into World War II.

## IMPRESSIVE EDIFICE

St. James United Methodist Church, shown in this aerial photograph taken in 1960, was built in 1927, replacing the edifice of the same name which stood catercornered across the Vermilion-Williams Streets intersection. In this view, Vermilion Street is at right, Williams Street in foreground and Walnut Street at left. The left wing of the church is the sanctuary; linking the two wings is the large community room. The church is of modified Gothic design in Bedford stone. Danville architect Harvey Skadden created the design for the church, considered by many experts to be the most beautiful edifice in the city.

## THEY PROTECTED KIDS

These stalwart youngsters were members of the Daniel School Safety Patrol, charged with protecting the safety of younger pupils at street crossings. They were, standing from left: Vincent Gondry, Bob Nabors, Bob Jarvis, Jim Stevens, Floyd Wear, Lawrence Thompson, Jim Gritton. Kneeling, from left, Jack Holdrieth, Bob Kegley, Richard Ireland, Bob Bivans, Bob Hill and Dick Wade.
*Photo courtesy of Bob Jarvis*

## SMALL BUT MIGHTY

This was the 1948 Daniel-Tilton-Grant-Hooton grade school football team which won four games and lost only one. Members were, front row, from left: James Bunting, O. Jae Michael, Dick Linderman, Johnny Broderick, Tommy Kelsheimer, Tommy Bann, Stanley Barker, Delbert Phillips, Bill DePratt, Richie Ireland and Bobby Jones, manager; back row, from left: Jerry Watson, Donald Underwood, Johnny Jones, Maxie Morgan, Joe Shaffer, Bob "Whiz Kid" Jarvis, Jack Klage, Bob Nabors, Dick "Fat" Ashby, Jimmy "Luke" Stevens, Herbert "Bones" Morgan. Harry Skadden, standing at extreme left, was the coach. *Photo courtesy of Bob Jarvis*

## DO YOU REMEMBER WHEN?

A majority of Danville residents were not born yet when this 1930 photograph was taken, looking north on Vermilion Street from Redden Square. But a substantial minority were either teenagers or young adults then and do remember how it was. Many buildings remain the same; only the retail establishments have changed. The Belmont Cafe, a popular eating place next to the courthouse, is gone but the site still is the location of a restaurant. F.W. Woolworth's store is gone, together with the professional offices in the three stories of the Daniel Building above it. But those stories have been covered with concrete and the lower floor transformed into an attractive and much-needed courthouse Annex. Although the streetcars are gone, along with the tracks, Danville still has a city-owned bus system. Will there be this much shopping activity again when the Vermilion Park-Mall is removed and traffic restored to Vermilion Street? Only time will tell.

## HOW THINGS HAVE CHANGED!

This was East Main Street in 1930 but the only thing recognizable today is the courthouse. No business remains from that era except Rhodes-Burford Furniture Store in the 100 block. But there were shoppers, on foot, in automobiles and streetcars. Note the spire of St. Patrick Catholic Church in the distance and, at the corner of Main and Hazel, the traffic signal located in the center of the street between the streetcar tracks. All the south side of Main to beyond the location of the old Meis Department Store (part of sign is showing) is covered by Towne Centre.

## THE WAY IT WAS

This familiar downtown landmark building has known many occupants, including the Vermilion County Farm Bureau and, when this 1925 picture was taken, the Danville Chamber of Commerce. For around 20 years, it was the location of the Danville Polyclinic. The exact date it was built is obscure but it probably was in the early post-World War I years. The building was raised to a 2½ story structure several years ago, now is occupied by offices of Danville Township.

## TURNING PAGES BACK

This is how St. Elizabeth Hospital looked about 1929. Its address was 600 Green Street; the street name was changed to Sager in later years to erase the stigma attached to the red-light district some blocks to the west. Elizabeth Street, where the Ford Model-T coupe is parked, was vacated in the 1950s when the next-to-last modernization and expansion took place. The cars parked in front of the hospital give a pretty good idea of when this photograph was taken; note the Ford Model-A coupe at the corner and the cabriolet style LaSalle sedan in front of the hospital entrance. The LaSalle, a companion car of the Cadillac, was the favorite car of Chicago gangsters in the last years of the Roaring Twenties.

## FIRST RESCUE SQUAD CAR

Capt. Frank Burton of the Danville Fire Department is at the wheel of Danville's first rescue squad car with equipment displayed beside it. The date of photograph is not known but probably was taken around 1930. Austin King, a large stockholder in the then-Second National Bank, gave the department one of his Lincolns which was subsequently converted for rescue work. King moved to New York City, where he was active as a financier until his death many years later.

The Danville Police Department in 1922 numbered only 29 men, which seems a little small. But motor power was beginning to bolster the manpower of walking a beat with the assignment of Officer Ted Prettyman as Danville's first motorcycle policeman. This photograph was taken in front of the main entrance to the City Hall on Walnut Street. The site is now covered by the municipal parking garage.

## MODERNIZATION BEGINS

Leins Restaurant on W. Main Street had an unusual slogan. It identified the owner as "The man who eats at his own restaurant." He had bumper stickers made up and gave them to his customers back in the 1920s. One of them later told of encountering in the wilds of West Texas a filling station attendant who, upon seeing the Danville plate above the license, brightened and said, "Oh, that's where the fellow lives that eats at his own restaurant!" Man at left above wearing a vest is the courageous restaurateur himself.

## INVENTOR'S DREAM COME TRUE

Fred Coffing was an automobile mechanic in Covington, Indiana, who thought there should be a better way to elevate cars so they could be worked on. So he tinkered with ideas during his spare time and came up with a revolutionary idea for a chain hoist. The model he constructed was workable and so effective there was immediate demand for it--so much so, in fact, that Coffing built this factory on the east side of Danville and went into production. Later, Coffing Hoist became a separate division of the Duff-Norton Corporation. This photograph is dated "about 1940."

## IT DID DOUBLE DUTY

This was the municipal water sprinkler. Pulled by a team of bay horses, it was used in the 1920s to keep dust down on city streets and also to cool hot paving surfaces. When not in use downtown, it was pressed into service to sprinkle the race track at the I&I Fairgrounds.

## EVERYTHING'S UP-TO-DATE...

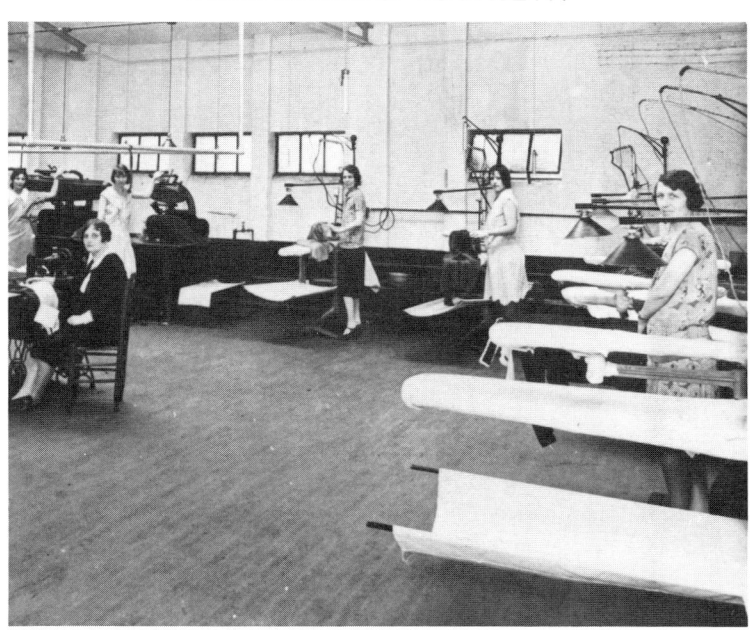

This was the finishing room of the Millikin Laundry and Dry Cleaners at 603 N. Vermilion St. after remodeling in 1929. The late Paul Millikin started the business in 1919 as a dry cleaning firm. It is still in existence; one of the few businesses begun in Danville in the 20th century to survive.

## WHEN A HARNESS SHOP WAS NEEDED

In June, 1945, *Commercial-News* reporter Jean Frobose, now Jean Frobose Byram, C-N editorial page editor, wrote a story about Morton Butler, harness maker. The picture above shows the interior of his shop at 19 N. Hazel Street. Butler is man at right; others in photograph are unidentified. He started his lifelong career as an apprentice to Amos Cowan, harness maker, in 1886. Note the horse collars suspended from the overhead rack and the iron-wheeled lawnmower in foreground. *Photo courtesy of Shirley Thiede.*

## MARKING THE WAY

This marker indicates the way Abraham Lincoln traveled to and from Danville as a circuit-riding lawyer between 1847 and 1859. Erected in 1921 by the Gov. Bradford Chapter, Daughters of the American Revolution, it stands atop the hill above Ellsworth Park at W. Main Street and N. Logan Avenue. Danville school children helped with the cost with their penny contributions.

The heroic statue of Victory, created by famed and sculptor Lorado Taft guards the northern approach to Victory Bridge, commonly known today as Memorial Bridge. The marble base of the monument enscrolls, the names of Vermilion County's 51 dead in World War I, with the figures of a Red Cross nurse and representatives of the armed forces in that conflict. Dedication of the monument and bridge was on November 11, 1922, fourth anniversary of Armistice Day. When a new span was built in the mid-1950s, the monument was moved to the land at the right side of the picture. The building at left in the picture was the Louis Rieker Grocery; structure at the right was headquarters of the Fairhall Elevator Company. The tracks in foreground carried passenger and freight trains of the Illinois Terminal (interurban) Railroad.

## PROUDLY SHE STANDS

## TRADE TOKENS

In 1964, Ore H. Vaketta was a perfectly content Westville auto dealer.

Then he was offered some trade tokens for an old truck.

He took them, thinking his son, Ore Jr., already a collector, might be interested in tokens as a side hobby.

What he didn't count on was himself. "I got so involved, so absorbed, I forgot it was supposed to be my son's hobby."

In 1974, more than 5,000 tokens later, the senior Vacketta wrote a book. *Trade Tokens of Illinois* was the first catalogue of trade tokens in Illinois. Thousands of tokens were listed, according to city of issue, composition, color, size and shape.

In Vacketta's book is the saga of C.S. Paxton, the Georgetown coal miner, who parlayed $185 in savings into a multimillion dollar business.

"He saved from his $2.50 a day salary, walking the combined 11 miles to and from his Georgetown home each day to save the 20-cent round trip car fare.

"He opened a combination grocery and dry goods store in Georgetown in 1903, then in July, 1919, decided to try a new idea, that of a cash and carry grocery." Before long, the store had become a chain.

The custom of trading with farmers for eggs, fruits, vegetables and poultry had some rough edges. Farmers sometimes had so much to sell they could not take all their credit in trade.

"Grab-It Here managers," Vacketta says, "bought from the farmers and paid them with tokens."

When the banks were closed in 1933, workers found paychecks bought neither food nor shelter. Ernest, C.S. Paxton's son, offered to cash paychecks in Grab-It Here tokens.

"The people got the food they needed. The Paxtons waited out the moratorium and, when it was ended, had $70,000 in paychecks to deposit."

*Taken from a story by Jean Byram, Commercial-News, February 3, 1974.*

Ore Vacketta of Westville, now a Danville real estate agent, displays some of the hundreds of trade tokens he has collected over a several-decade span. The tokens were prepared for merchants to give to their customers either as bonuses or lures and could be redeemed in trade only at the dispensing source.

## HISTORIC CORNER

This historic northeast corner of Hazel and North Streets for nearly 25 years was the site of the Terrace Theater, Danville's largest movie showhouse. When it was torn down, a grocery store building was erected in 1934, with its architecture influenced by the Chicago World's Fair (1933-34). After its first occupant, the Oakley grocery chain of Terre Haute, Indiana, consolidated with Kroger's, the Grab-It-Here Company of Danville obtained the building for one of its stores. The site now is a municipal parking lot. Looking north on Hazel Street, the sign of the Marlatt School of Dancing can be seen and at the corner with Harrison Street, the Illinois National Guard Armory.

## DARING YOUNG MAN AND HIS FLYING MACHINE

Clarence Carter, who had a lifetime love affair with airplanes, shows off his Waco 10, two-place biplane in this 1930 photograph at the Chamber of Commerce Airport east of Danville. Carter, who owned the Modern Machine Shop, was an engineering genius who held many patents for intricate packaging and filling devices used in industry and was a pioneer in the development of the local aerosol industry. He was a promoter of the Vermilion County Airport, served on the board of the Airport Authority and was honored by the designation of the landing strip area as Clarence Carter Field.

## USHERING IN A NEW ERA

In 1928, the Illinois Chamber of Commerce sponsored a tour of state airports. Members of the state organization met Danville notables and fliers at the Chamber of Commerce Airport, east of the city on what was then Illinois Route 10, now U.S. Highway 136. Standing center in a white suit is Camlin Quincy, president of the Illinois Chamber of Commerce. The tall man immediately to his left is M.C. Meigs, publisher of the Chicago Herald-Examiner, for whom Chicago's Meigs Airport is named. Next to Quincy is Mrs. Gene (Katherine) Lamm, Danville's first woman flier. Others, from left, (all from Danville) are Hervey Parker, Byron Bilderback, Jack M. Williams, Danville Mayor Henry Hulce, Harold Johnson, Russ Roettger, Peter Britz, Dean Huber, president of the Danville Chamber, and Gene Lamm. Britz and Lamm, both enthusiastic pilots, were killed in plane crashes near Danville several years later.

## FUN FOR THE KIDS

Children looked forward every year to the Rotary Club's Christmas party—and the host-members got a kick out of it, too. This photograph was taken about 1929; the theater closed, except for use by large public gatherings, the following year. During its heyday it booked many nationally-known vaudeville performers, including Al Jolson. Jolson and Alice White starred in *Show Girl*, the first talkie seen at the Terrace by Danville people in 1928.

A LIFETIME IN SAME HOUSE

In this picture taken around 1920, Mrs. G. Haven Stephens, whose maiden name was Elizabeth Fairlee Stewart, stands in front of the William F. Stewart home. She resided in this gracious home, built in 1878, for 92 years. It was located on the southeast corner of Hazel and Williams Streets, just north of the present-day Korean-Vietnam War Memorial and across the street from the Pape Mortuary. Her husband, a dentist, was secretary of the Masonic bodies in Danville for many years and was a past master of Illinois Masons. *Photo courtesy of Haven Stephens*

The occasion was the organization and founding of Danville's community theater. The date was December 1, 1936. The founders and charter members of Danville's Red Mask Players are pictured from left, seated: Katherine Robison (later Katherine Gerrard), Mrs. Kathryn Randolph, director of Red Mask plays for the first 30 years, Mrs. Gene Bennett, Betty Wilson Ewers, Robert L. Horney, Mrs. Virginia Thrasher, Miss Esther Cowan, Mrs. Joanna Jones Bishop. Standing, from left, are Leland Thrasher, Tep Wright and Clinton Sandusky.

RED MASK FOUNDERS

# HELEN MORGAN

(The following is excerpted from the April 5 (Centennial), 1966, Edition of the *Commercial-News*)

The song is ended but the legend lives on. Helen Morgan was 41 when she died. She had been famous for half her life but no one ever really had known her.

Her name was news and columnists, in the unending competition for reader interest, often had distorted the facts of her life or invented some.

Even the recorded facts don't solve the riddle that was Helen Morgan. What was the spark that set people afire when they heard her sing?

Weavers of words coined phrases to describe her appeal—the Camille of the Piano"; a "Raffish Nightingale," and a name perhaps most revealing—"Lady Bountiful."

Stories of her lifelong generosity are legion. Fellow performers down on their luck, relatives, friends . . . anyone she knew who needed help, received it. Strangers were often recipients of her impulsive giving—a checkroom girl given $100 on Christmas Eve; a young, struggling actress draped in Miss Morgan's ermine, and a scrubwoman's burdens made lighter by a large gift of money.

Born in Danville in the family home on E. Madison Street, Helen and her family left town when she was three and returned three years later. She attended first grade at Grant School, later went to Jackson School and then Washington School.

Her mother taught Sunday School and Helen sang in a mission located over the Cal Jamison grocery at Third and S. Gilbert streets in South Danville, which later became the South Side Church of Christ.

The family moved again and later Helen returned for a short time. She had many friends here . . . who still remember fondly the young Helen. In 1987, these include Mrs. Gladys Walker and Mrs. Disa Jamison Maxwell.

Helen and her widowed mother moved to Chicago when she was in her late teens. She didn't launch her career as an entertainer until she was clerking in a Chicago department store and singing in small cabarets.

Drama critic Amy Leslie, taken by Helen's personality, sent her to New York with a letter of introduction to Flo Ziegfeld. The great producer was less than thrilled with Helen's voice, gave her a job in the back row of the chorus in *Louis XIV*. Helen didn't like it and quit in a couple of days.

During the lean days that followed, Helen got a job singing at Billy Rose's Backstage Club. It was here, the story is told, that the famed writer, Ring Lardner, lifted her up to sit on the grand piano so that the crowd could see and hear her (she was barely five feet tall). The success of this gesture caused her to adopt it as a characteristic . . . one she ever after was identified with.

Whatever the catalyst—suddenly there was Helen, riding the crest of fame in the Roaring Twenties and Turbulent Thirties. She played in Ziegfeld's *Follies* and *Sally*; George White's *Scandals*; appeared in *Sweet Adeline*; made several successful appearances in London and Paris, and responded to the call of Hollywood, where she appeared in many movies and was a featured radio singer.

Her greatest stage role, which brought her lasting renown, was as Julie in Ziegfeld's *Show Boat*. In night clubs she had her greatest popularity, however, where her never big voice was just right and where she "hushed everything from the ringside to the kitchen ranges." Four New York City clubs bore her name in succession—Helen Morgan's 54th Street Club; Chez Helen Morgan; Helen Morgan's Summer Home, and The House of Morgan.

As the Thirties ended, her star had dimmed, her popularity waned. But she couldn't rest—she had a compulsion to work. In 1941, she married Lloyd Johnson in Los Angeles, then went back to Chicago for an engagement at the Chez Paree, where her final illness overtook her. She underwent surgery at Henrotin Hospital and on Wednesday, October 8, 1941, she died. Her mother and husband were at her bedside and so in spirit were millions of admirers.

The story of the little girl who sang in the choir of a South Danville mission and rose to world fame continues to stir hearts.

She sang, *I've Got Sand in My Shoes.*

Probably.

But she also had a magic in her voice that continues to vibrate across the years . . .

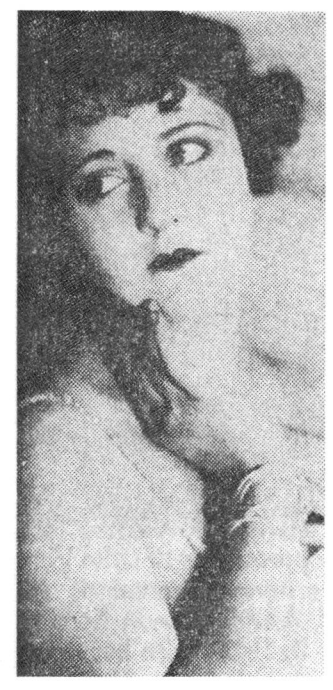

WHERE IT STARTED

It was on the second floor of the Cal Jamison Grocery, Gilbert and First Streets in South Danville, that Helen Morgan, star of Broadway and Hollywood, started her career. The Danville native sang for services of a church mission which evolved into the South Side Church of Christ. Mrs. Disa Jamison Maxwell, who was still living in 1987, was a girlhood chum of Miss Morgan.

WHAT'S IN A NAME?

In a contest to name this hotel, built in the early 1930s, the winner proposed "Harwal," combining the first three letters of the streets forming the intersection, Harrison and Walnut. At first, the Harwal offered transient room service but now is occupied by permanent residents. The photograph was taken in 1969. Note the yesteryear style boulevard light on the curb at right. It is the only one of its kind in Danville.

Although this photograph was taken in 1943, the I&I Swimming Pool, located on the fairgrounds of the same name on Fairchild Street, was the most popular place in town during the summer months of the 1920s through the 1950s. Much of the site of the fairgrounds is now covered by apartment buildings of the Danville Housing Authority for financially-disadvantaged residents.

HAVEN ON A HOT DAY

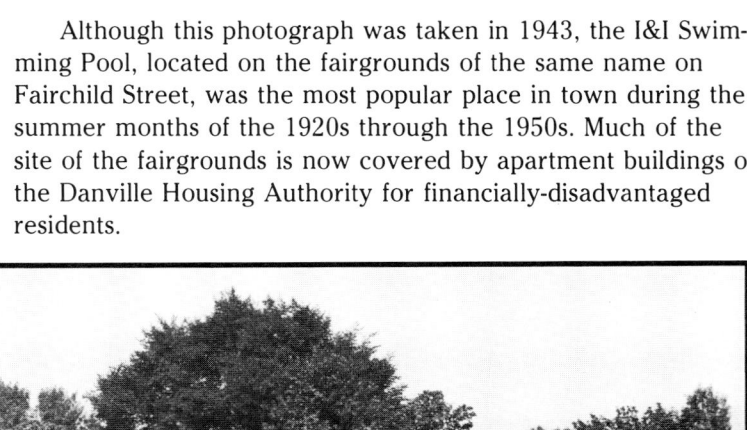

These horse-drawn delivery wagons of the Herendeen Milling Company & Bakery, located on S. Hazel Street at Green Street, made it possible for customers to have fresh-baked bread and rolls for breakfast every day if they so desired. Danville dairies likewise delivered milk and cream. These two services contributed to older residents' fond memories of "the good old days."

BREAD FOR BREAKFAST

THE OLD GIVES WAY TO THE NEW

Although this was a posed shot, it seems that a Beard Ice Company truck is overtaking a company team and wagon at the loading dock on College Street. The year was 1932 when trucks were taking over home deliveries.

## FREE CAMPING ATTRACTS

![camping scene]

Strange as it may seem to young people today, the free campgrounds in the southwestern part of Garfield Park attracted many people who put up tents, canopy shelters or who even came in the early version of motor homes (see pioneering model in background in this 1925 picture). During the Great Depression of the 1930s, many jobless people took advantage of the chance to stay three days or even for extended stays by obtaining a special permit from City Hall.

These members of the Danville Consistory were ready to depart for a Masonic meeting in Springfield when this picture was taken in 1925. In background is their chartered Illinois Traction System car which could traverse easily and comfortably the 125-mile nonstop distance in approximately two hours.

## SPECIAL TRIP

# HOLIDAY BLUES

Passage of more than 40 years has not alleviated the Christmas holiday mailing crunch, as this December, 1946, photograph on the steps of the former post office clearly shows. Letter carriers, numbered, were: (1) Donald Heidrick; (2) Willis McMaster; (3) Steve Arnold; (4) Cecil Crane; (5) Sam Smart; (6) Leo Soneson; (7) Elby Price; (8) Ace Wright; (9) Fred Peterson; (10) Walter Jenkins; (11) Joseph Walters; (12) Charles O'Neal; (13) Carl Kramer; (14) John Arnold; (15) Louis Decker; (16) Jack Hathaway; (17) Joe Kaneen; (18) William O'Neil; (19) Nelson Lewis; (20) Sam Lind; (21) Paul Blair; (22) Herman Radloff; (23) Harry Rindt.
*Photo courtesy of Willis McMaster*

## SMALL BOY, LARGE COAT

It must have been a cold May, back in 1927, if the long, heavy coat little Billy Nasser is wearing is any indication. Note absence of traffic signals at Gilbert-Williams intersection in background as automobile turns south off Williams from the east. Also note the gateman's tower at the Big Four tracks; it was this railroad employee's duty to activate levers that would lower and raise crossing gates when a train approached.
*Photo courtesy of William Nasser*

## CELEBRATING A CENTURY

This is a float used in the Vermilion County Centennial Celebration parade in 1926. The photograph was snapped while the procession was en route north on Vermilion Street in front of the Sandusky Furniture Store. The site later was occupied by the Block & Kuhl and Carson Pirie Scott department stores and, in 1987, is the location of offices of the Illinois Department of Children and Family Services. The float bore a replica of Danville's first school—in the 10-by-12-foot log Haworth's smoke house on the north west corner of the public square.

## EARLY RADIO

When WDAN, Danville's first radio station, went on the air in 1938, studios were located on the lower level of the Hotel Wolford. In this photograph, taken around 1940, Carl "Bud" Sunkel reads a commercial, while Leo Shapiro (now deceased) provides background music. Man in background is Norlyn Dossey, recently retired from Warner Cable of Danville. Sunkel is still active in radio in the Danville area. Note wire basket of glass milk bottles on top of piano. These were the distinctive cream-top bottles of Bredehoft (later Meadow Gold) Dairy. Cream rose to the top and could be poured out without mixing with milk by using a special spoon which blocked narrow opening to lower part of bottle. Milk was delivered to customers door-to-door by horse-drawn enclosed wagons, later trucks. During World War II, horses were pressed back into service.

In their snappy uniforms with plumed hussar caps, the American Legion Curtis G. Redden Post 210 Drum and Bugle Corps made a thrilling appeal to the eyes and ears of crowds at parades and large public events. In this picture the corps poses proudly as the 1937 Class A state champion of the Legion's Department of Illinois. The man designated by an X on his cap plume is Edwin M. Stuebe.
*Photo courtesy of Harriet Pashe*

## SNAPPY OUTFIT

## GONE BUT NOT FORGOTTEN

This section of the west side of Vermilion Street's 100 block survives only in this photograph or the memories of older residents. The Sears, Roebuck & Company store now occupies most of the site; the east-west alley from Walnut Street would be just about in the middle of the store. The DeLuxe Restaurant, formerly Sanichas, moved around the corner next door to the *Commercial-News* and opened for business on Mother's Day, 1939. Next door south to the restaurant in this picture was the McMillan Hat Shop, the Kiningham Boot Shop. The Colony Shop, across the alley, sold women's apparel, then came Pittsburgh Plate Glass Company, which also sold paints. Next, to the south, were Jenkins Cigar Store, with bowling alleys on the second floor; a shoe repair shop; Ike S. Levin store for men; Spivey Shoe Store, Plaster Drug Store, and, in a tiny, narrow space, Gallaher's Tik-Tok Shop, watch and clock repairs. The first, second and second-floor annex of the Temple Building were occupied by Montgomery Ward Company store. Walgreen Drugs can be identified in the distance, across North Street.

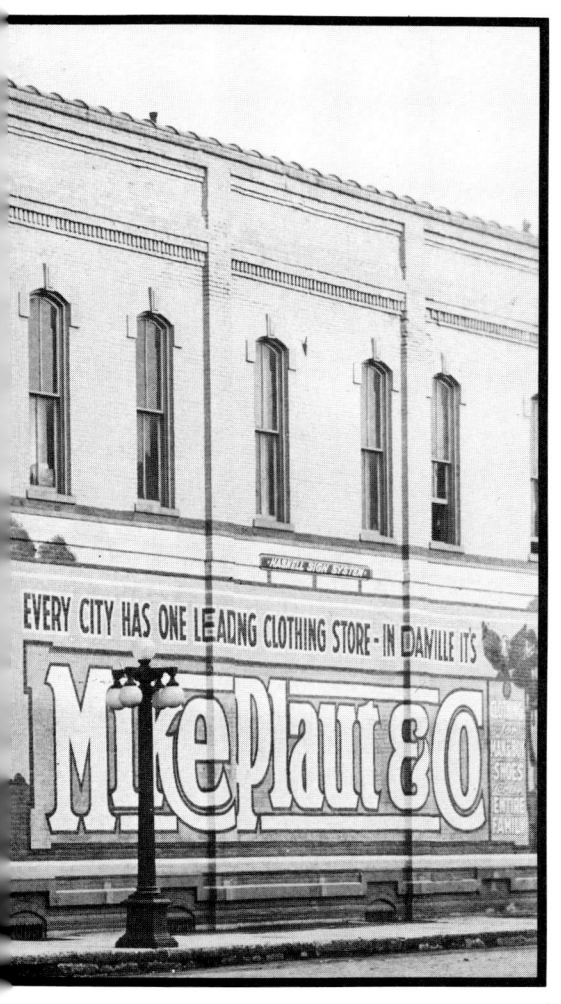

## SPACIOUS STORE

Mike Plaut's men's clothing store, on the northwest corner of Main and Hazel streets, was one of Danville's leading haberdasheries for many years. Note the fancy five-globe street lights in this 1925 photograph. Plaut's home occupied the half-block (in depth) behind the Cannon mansion on Vermillion Street, fronting on Walnut Street and bordering Cannon Alley.

## SCOPES TRIAL

Neighbors who noticed Danville High School senior John Scopes go in and out of this home at 122 Minnesota Avenue in 1919 could not dream that in a scant six years he would be the central figure in a trial that would make newspaper headlines from coast to coast.

Thomas Scopes, his father, was a machinist at the Oaklawn Shops of the C&EI Railroad, having transferred some four years earlier from Salem, Illinois, birthplace of a prominent political figure, William Jennings Bryan, destined to play a prominent role in John Scopes' life.

But the Scopes family was not destined to remain long in Danville after young John's graduation. They moved to Kentucky, where John entered the University of Kentucky at Lexington.

He graduated with a degree in biology and began looking for a job as a teacher. He found one at Dayton, Tennessee, High School where he went to work in the fall of 1924.

A playwright once described Dayton as "the buckle on the Bible Belt." Needless to say, Dayton residents were sincere churchgoers with a fervent, unswerving fundamentalist belief in the Bible as it was written. Young Scopes, who had just as fervent a belief in evolution, was bound to get in trouble.

A few of the more militant parents, convinced that Scopes was teaching evolution to their children in violation of state law, had him arrested. Thus began the events that came to a head in the summer of 1925. And that was when John Scopes, DHS Class of 1919, became John Scopes, Number 1 U.S. newsmaker.

To Bible fundamentalists both in Dayton and across the nation, Scopes was Satan personified for daring to deny creation. To those who held that the Bible's language was symbolic, the young teacher was the David of intellectual thinking challenging the Goliath of narrow and unimaginative dogma.

The trial shaped up as a contest between conservative and liberal thinking. The local prosecutors were only too happy when William Jennings Bryan, unofficial leader of the fundamentalists, volunteered his services to head the prosecution. The evolutionist side was cheered when Chicago's famed Clarence Darrow, an avowed agnostic and brilliant defense lawyer, offered to defend Scopes.

The courthouse in Dayton was stifling in mid-summer heat so proceedings were moved outdoors onto the lawn. It was high theater. Press representatives assembled from across the nation, including the famed H.L. Mencken of the *Baltimore Sun*, whose acid-flecked stories showed him clearly on Scopes' side.

He was about the only one. The partisan crowd adored Bryan and despised Darrow. On debating points alone, Darrow made Bryan look bad.

Nevertheless, the July 24 verdict was foreordained: "Guilty." The judge announced that Scopes was fined $100. Darrow immediately advised the court that the verdict would be appealed and that Scopes had no intention of ever paying the fine.

He never did. A higher Tennessee court found for Scopes on grounds of technical errors in the trial.

The former Danville young man lost his job, of course, and moved to Louisiana, where he worked the rest of his life as an accountant for an oil company. He died several years later at a comparatively early age.

The final irony of the Scopes "monkey trial" (so-called because of one widespread evolutionist belief that man is descended from the apes) was the post-trial finding that Scopes had not reached in his textbook the passages that dealt with evolution, hence never had taught it!

## PRIDE OF THE FORTIES

This attractive structure is the former Lincoln School, built in 1941 in the area bounded on the east by Chandler Street, on the west by Grant Street and on the north by Williams Street. It replaced the original Lincoln School which stood on the site for many decades. This picture was taken in February, 1987, shortly before the school was closed as surplus to the needs of School District 118. The school and its predecessor building were attended by several generations of Tinchertown residents.

BIG EMPLOYER

During a near-half century of existence, the Oaklawn Shops of the C&EI Railroad played a major role in the economy of Danville. At peak production in the 1920s, as many as 1,700 were employed there, building and repairing passenger cars and locomotives. Counting maintenance men and road crews, office workers, rail yard workers, passenger depot personnel of the C&EI, the Wabash, the New York Central, the Big Four and the Illinois Terminal Railroad (interurban), railway employment at one time was approximately 3,000. This bird's-eye view photograph was taken in 1940; the sparsely developed area to the north and west indicates the considerable growth of the city in the past 47 years.

If this 1938 picture were to come alive it would thrill the hearts of railroad buffs. It's "The Dixieland," the C&EI Railroad's Train No. 92, just north of Vincennes, Indiana, and headed for Chicago by way of Danville. Steam engine 1018 is pulling a baggage car and nine passenger coaches at a stop-action speed probably in excess of 60 miles an hour. This was one of several C&EI Florida trains. Engineer Zack Laking leans out of window of the locomotive cab.

A BEAUTY TO BUFFS

## WILLIAM R. HUMRICHOUSE - AIR FORCE

Danville's most decorated Army Air Forces flier in World War II was Maj. William R. Humrichouse. And, ironically, he was killed in an automobile accident near an American air base in England on Feb. 16, 1953.

Born in Danville April 15, 1916, he was graduated from Danville High School and attended the University of Illinois for three years before enrolling in the air cadet program.

Maj. Humrichouse was stationed at Pearl Harbor when the Japanese launched their sneak attack. As a member of a B-17 bomber squadron, he participated in the crucial battle of Midway. In later action in the Southwest Pacific, he flew numerous missions against enemy ships and aircraft installations.

During his 13 years of service, he was awarded the Silver Star with Oak Leaf Cluster, the Distinguished Flying Cross with Oak Leaf Cluster and the Air Medal with two Oak Leaf Clusters.

After the war, he was stationed again at Pearl Harbor until he was named Vice President Alben Barkley's personal pilot, a position he held for two years.

## ROBERT B. CHAPMAN - ARMY

He was only 24 when he was killed in action but the name of one of Danville's most illustrious war heroes is perpetuated in the name above the door: "Robert B. Chapman Army Reserve Center" at 2409 E. Main Street.

Capt. Chapman died leading his men against a Japanese strong-point at Tamagan, Mindanao, Philippine Islands, on June 24, 1945. The citation accompanying the Silver Star he was awarded posthumously notes his "fearless courage, superior leadership and inspiration." His death was not in vain for the operation crushed enemy resistance.

Born in Danville Jan. 12, 1921, Chapman was graduated in 1939 from Danville High School where he was a cheerleader. He enlisted the same year. He also won the Purple Heart and Bronze Star medals.

## JOSEPH TAYLOR - NAVY

Few men ever win the Navy Cross, second only to the Medal of Honor. The highest ranking naval officer in Vermillion County history, Joseph Taylor, was awarded three.

Taylor, a native of Central Park, was graduated from Danville High School in 1923 and from Annapolis in 1927.

He became a flier after graduation and was commanding a torpedo plane squadron on the carrier *Yorktown* in the early days of World War II. Taylor's squadron sank an enemy seaplane carrier in March, 1942, and he won his first Navy Cross. Two months later, he received a second cross during the Battle of the Coral Sea.

Taylor's finest hour came later in the war when he was executive officer of the *Benjamin Franklin*. While 60 miles off Japan, an enemy bomber slipped through the clouds and scored two direct hits on the carrier. As second in command, Taylor assumed charge from the disabled captain and directed restoring the crippled carrier winning his third Navy Cross.

Taylor was a rear admiral when he retired in 1958. He died May 4, 1963.

## KENNETH BAILEY - MARINES

The safety of several American posts in the Pacific Theater was dependent on a victory on Guadalcanal Island late in September, 1942. A Danville man, Marine Maj. Kenneth Bailey, probably was more instrumental in getting that win than anyone else.

Maj. Bailey gave his life in that epic struggle. But his record had become almost legendary before that morning of September 27, 1942, when he fell, the victim of a Japanese machine gunner.

In one battle in defense of strategic Henderson Field, he was credited with accounting for 32 of the enemy. The air field was the prize on this Japanese-held island.

His widow accepted a posthumous Congressional Medal of Honor. Bailey also had won the Silver Star and Purple Heart. A destroyer was named after him, as was a road at the U.S Naval Academy in Annapolis, Maryland.

Bailey was a native of Oklahoma who came to Danville as a child. He attended Oaklawn School, graduated from Danville High School and worked his way through the University of Illinois, where he received a Marine Corps commission upon graduation.

---

## FOURTH BRIDGE

The present Memorial Bridge, carrying S. Gilbert Street and Illinois Route 1 over the Vermilion River, built in 1956, is the fourth span in the location in less than 100 years. It replaced the first memorial Bridge, dedicated in 1923, which had succeeded the iron bridge, built in 1895. That span had replaced the old Red Bridge (covered), erected in 1857. Before that travelers crossed the river on a ferry. Note in left foreground the deteriorating stone abutment of the Red Bridge. The statue of Victory and World War I monument supporting it, also dedicated in 1922, was moved from the middle of the roadway to adjacent ground to the west when this bridge was built.

## LAKE VERMILION DAM

Pictured is a view of the big Inter-State Water Company dam from the downstream side shortly after Lake Vermilion, formed by damming the North Fork River, had filled in 1925. The engineers' report adds this information: "The dam impounds a body of water now called Lake Vermilion which is about 1,000 acres in extent. The lake is between 4 and 5 miles long and seven-eighths of a mile across at the widest part. When filled to spillway level (elevation 567 feet), there is impounded about 2.6 billion gallons. The drainage area above the dam is 267 square miles." Erosion of contiguous land and siltation have reduced the reservoir capacity in the 62 years since the dam was built and the lake first filled.

## LONG-TIME SURVIVOR

This bridge over the channel of the North Fork River in Lake Vermilion was in place for more than 60 years, being replaced in 1985 by the modern Dallas Bowman Bridge, honoring a leading environmentalist's memory. The area on either side of the bridge was the ancient site of the village of Denmark. The ascending road in the background is Denmark Hill, leading to the junction of Winter and Logan Avenues.

## GOING BACK 65 YEARS

## CLAWING AT THE EARTH

This was the scene of strip mining operations back in 1922. The loading shovel is filling the last of a string of cars with the shale and dirt from the overburden removed at United Electric Mine No. 1, west of Danville. This was the first step prior to actual removal of coal. These excavations now are filled with water, forming the many lakes and ponds in Kickapoo State Park.

This huge stripping shovel is removing the overburden—sometimes nearly 70 feet in depth—above the coal seams. The photograph was taken in 1922 at the United Electric Coal Company Mine No. 1 west of Danville. After the coal had been removed, the excavations were abandoned and left to fill with water from rainfall and from natural springs uncovered in stripping. The rest is the many ponds and lagoons that now dot Kickapoo State Park.

This dragline of Fairview Collieries Corporation is getting final assembly touches before going into service at the Harmattan Mine west of Danville. This picture, taken October 18, 1948, gives some idea of the dragline's enormous size and capability. The cab, housing the electrically-powered motors and complicated controls, is as large as a two-story apartment building. The bucket, at left, could scoop up 30 cubic yards of overburden at a single pass.

## PREPARING A GIANT

## IMPRESSIVE LAYOUT

This was the nerve center of Ayrshire Collieries' Harmattan strip mine west of Danville. After the coal was stripped it was loaded into huge Diesel-engine trucks each with a capacity of 40 tons. As an example of these behemoths' size, each tire stood seven feet tall and cost $2,500 40 years ago. The coal was brought to a conveyor belt which took it inside the seven-story processing plant (white building in center foreground). All the coal adjacent to the plant and at some considerable distance--20 millions tons--was stripped in 20 years of operation between 1947 and 1967. Many of the excavations left when the coal was removed have filled with water from natural springs, forming ponds which have been stocked with fish. Fishing is open to the public with a permit from the coal company. Around 1,500 acres of land were purchased by a Danville man who developed the area for homesites at the water's edge.

## PLANT OF MANY NAMES

This meat packing plant on S. Washington Avenue always had that type of business but under many names. When this 1944 photograph was taken, it was Rose Packing Company. Earlier, a firm known as the Baum Packing Company occupied the plant and before that the Campbell Brothers Packing Company. Later, the William L. Davies Packing Company was the owner-operator.

## CHAPTER V

# RECOVERY
# AND
# CHANGE

## 1951 - PRESENT

As the 20th century passed the halfway point, Danville faced a different kind of future with confidence.

Many of its young adults had been born during World War I or immediately afterward. As teen-agers, they had suffered, along with their elders, the hardships of the Great Depression of the 1930s.

Many bright young people had to forego a college education, opting instead for jobs in a gradually recovering economy.

But World War II broke the jobs market wide open for both young men and young women, in uniform and out. And when it was ended, the GI Bill of Rights enabled millions of veterans to obtain the college education denied to them earlier.

The self-denial of the war years had created a great demand for everything—houses, automobiles, clothing, furniture, appliances and all manner of both necessary and luxury items. And the beneficent effect of this touched Danville.

Thus, the three-eighths of a century between 1950 and 1987 has seen dramatic changes in this community, affecting the lives of its citizens in countless ways.

Some critics, basing their opinion on a slight decline in overall population, have rushed to judgment. They charge, untruthfully, that "nothing ever happens in Danville," that "you don't see any progress in this town."

The pictorial history of Danville during the past 3.7 decades, as depicted in this Chapter 5, is evidence enough to give the lie to this claim.

Old streets have been repaired, some principal thoroughfares have been widened. New streets have been built. Key intersections have been enlarged. Old highway bridges have been replaced.

In the area of local government, Danville built a new City Hall and three fire stations—on N. Vermilion, N. Griffin and Bremer Avenue—plus a parking garage and a parking deck downtown.

The Danville Police Department joined the Vermilion County Sheriff's Department in sharing headquarters in the new Public Safety Building. The jail in this building, one of the highest-rated in the nation, has replaced the century-old county jail.

The 75-year-old Vermilion County Courthouse has undergone extensive interior renovation and improvement. The old Daniel Building across Vermilion Street from the courthouse was donated to the county by a Champaign family; at far less cost than constructing a new building, this structure has been remodeled to provide space for many county offices hitherto crowded into the central building.

A civic center, named for the late David S. Palmer, Danville mayor during its construction, was built.

For 20 years, starting in 1967, the Vermilion Street-Park Mall was a closed off portion of that principal thoroughfare, extending north from Redden Square to Harrison Street. It was a pleasant grass-covered area, adorned with trees, shrubbery, flowers, fountains, sculpture, benches and some playground features for children.

But downtown merchants, faced with ever-stiffening competition from outlying shopping plazas and the Village Mall, began to view the development as a sort of whited sepulchre. They argued that loss of vehicular traffic past their stores, along with a lack of proximity parking, was ruining business. As a result, the city agreed to demolish the mall, put Vermilion Street back as a roadway and offer limited free parking at curbside. The project, begun in mid-summer of 1987, is scheduled to be completed in time for the Christmas shopping season.

Meanwhile, the shopping plaza concept has grown rapidly. The enclosed Village Mall, north of the central city, has achieved regional mall status with the addition in the past couple of years of two major anchor stores and many smaller stores.

K-mart and Holiday Square are the other outlying plazas but downtown has a counterpart in Towne Centre, located in the old urban renewal area south of Redden Square. Towne Centre also has an office building which is home both to the First National Bank and the Danville Area Chamber of Commerce and several professional offices.

All three major banks have built drive-in banking complexes in various parts of the city. Lake Shore National Bank came into being in the north end of the city. Bank of Danville was established, then merged with the old Second National Bank which, after major interior renovation and a new front, acquired a new name: First Midwest Bank/Danville.

Foreign competition has hurt major Danville industries, helping to raise the city's unemployment rate to a current 13-plus percent, highest since the 1930s. One, Hyster Company, might have left Danville had it not been for the financial help provided by the state, city and Danville Township governments. Bohn, Tee-Pak, ESCO and General Motors have survived cutbacks; General Electric Company sold its local plant to Valmont Electric in August, 1987. But a number of firms have located here, notably, Quaker Oats, Anchor Hocking and Wyman-Gordon.

The new Danville Correctional Center is a high medium security state prison. The site, east of Danville near 74 Eastgate industrial park, was selected on Sept. 26, 1982, with groundbreaking on Oct. 27, 1983, and dedication on Oct. 9, 1985. The first inmates were received on Oct. 10, 1985, and the total late in 1987 was 926.

The Chamber of Commerce changed its name to Danville Area Chamber of Commerce and added a dimension to its services: The Vistors and Convention Bureau. The Danville Economic Development Corporation has fought to keep the city's name in contention, even overseas, when there is a chance of locating an industry or business here.

New churches have been built, including First Church of the Nazarene, Free Methodist, Northland Christian Church, the Church of Jesus Christ of Latter-Day Saints (Mormon) and Assembly of God, plus the Second Church of Christ at the edge of the city. They join such long-established places of worship as Congregation Israel, St. Paul Catholic, Allen Chapel A.M.E. and Assembly of God, all of which have undergone renovation or expansion.

Danville Area Community College has expanded with new buildings and adult non-credit courses. At a lower level, Hope Christian High School has come into being and many new public schools.

A Family YMCA has been built. Red Mask Players, Danville Light Opera, Danville Symphony Orchestra and Danville Art League are doing well. There is a new post office.

And, finally, Danville is getting a new form of city government. Back in 1927, citizens voted to end the mayor-aldermanic system, which called for one alderman in each of 10 wards. In its place came the city commission structure of four persons elected at large, plus a mayor. Each commissioner had charge of a specific department: Finance, streets, public property (parks) and public health and safety (garbage collection and fire protection). But early in 1987, Danville blacks filed a suit, charging that the federal Civil Rights Act was being violated in that the commission form of government discriminated against blacks. In a controversial compromise approved by the federal court, the incumbent commission agreed to restoration of the mayor-aldermanic government, held a primary and, on September 15, elected 14 aldermen from seven racially-balanced wards, plus a mayor. In a closely contested race, Gerald Arnholt, a former city commissioner, was defeated by Bob Jones, incumbent county treasurer.

One hundred sixty years after its founding, Danville can look to the future with the kind of confidence that inspired its spiritual ancestors to build a city in a howling wilderness.

---

## WHERE TRAINS, PASSENGERS MET

This is an aerial view of the C&EI Railroad Passenger Station, taken in the 1950s. Built in 1916-1917, the depot, with its vaulted ceiling waiting room, mahogany benches, tiled floor and adjacent restaurant, rivaled, in miniature, the stations of much larger cities. The train on the track, headed north, might have been one of several crack Florida trains serving the city during the heyday of passenger service, such as the *Dixie Flyer, Dixieland* and the *Humming Bird*. Travelers could board a train in the morning, breakfast in the dining car and arrive at Chicago's Dearborn Street Station two hours later. They had the option of later afternoon, early and late evening times for the return trip. By the mid-to-late Sixties, passenger train service in Danville had virtually disappeared from all railroads.

## DAN BECKWITH BRIDGE

Although the City Council hasn't taken formal action to designate it, the span carrying W. Main Street over the North Fork River in Ellsworth Park is known to local history buffs as the Dan Beckwith Bridge. The name was the popular choice in competition conducted by the Heritage, official magazine of the Vermilion County Museum Society. As this photograph, taken in the mid-Fifties, indicates, the bridge is built uphill to join the intersection of W. Main Street and N. and S. Logan Avenue.

## CITY HALL

This two-story building at the corner of Hazel and Seminary streets, a block east of N. Vermilion Street, was constructed in 1954 to become Danville's new City Hall. It replaced the old City Hall in the unit block of N. Walnut Street, built in 1896, and also housed Central Fire Station (large door openings in center of building). Additional space was obtained when the Police Department, at far right of building, moved to the new Public Safety Building, and a new fire station was built on N. Griffin Street. The Plan Department moved to the space vacated by the police and a ground level City Council chamber was built, leaving extra space in its former second floor location.

## PARKING MADE EASY

Downtown parking congestion was eased in 1958 with the construction of this four-story municipal parking garage. Located in the unit block of N. Walnut Street, it occupies the sites of the old City Hall and an open-air parking lot and has a capacity of 240 vehicles. Access is from both Walnut and W. North streets. Many downtown workers lease space by the month.

NOT THE VILLAGE SMITHY

This photograph of the interior of the Fischer Theater is sure to evoke a pang from older movie fans who loved its atmosphere of elegance and near-perfect acoustics. Original seating capacity was around 900, including main floor, mezzanine, balcony and six boxes. When Kerasotes theater chain purchased the Fischer in 1971, new seats were installed on the main floor boosting capacity there to around 600 and the balance of the seating capacity was dispensed with. The theater finally was closed in the early 1980s and efforts to restore it (Kerasotes has offered to give the building to the city) have failed thus far. The Fischer is the modern version of Heinley's Grand Opera, built more than a century ago.

A far cry from the old smithy where horses were shod and metal tires shrunk on buggy wheels is this forge in the C&EI Railroad's Oaklawn Shops. Blacksmith Carl Voss, center, is shaping a piece of metal in this 1953 photograph. Workers with him are unidentified. Voss worked at the shops from 1913 to 1953. Peak employment there was 1,700 in the 1920s.
*Photo courtesy of Nancy Voss*

ELEGANCE OF YESTERYEAR

## MCKINLEY SCHOOL

McKinley School, located in Vermilion Heights, was opened in August of 1980 to serve the needs of the moderately, severely and profoundly handicapped students in Vermillion County. Students are eligible to attend from the age of three to 21. Many McKinley students are referred from the Developmental Learning Center or the Early Childhood Program. Steve Johns is the principal.

## NORTH RIDGE SCHOOL

North Ridge Middle School at 1619 N. Jackson Street was dedicated as a junior high school when it was built back in 1962. But the concept changed and it reverted to middle school status, that is, serving children in the sixth, seventh and eighth grades. North Ridge's student population of 875 is up this year because East Park, hitherto a middle school. has changed to kindergarten through five, putting a heavier student load on the two remaining middle schools. The faculty of 60 is headed by Principal Phil Smith.

## NORTHEAST SCHOOL

Northeast School was built in 1953 at 1330 E. English Street as a kindergarten through 6th grade elementary building. In 1980, when District 118 developed middle schools, the building housed kindergarten through 5th grade. In 1987, Northeast opened as a "Young Learners' School." It houses Early Childhood, CARE (Children at Risk Educationally), kindergarten and first grade classes. There are 400 students with 32 teachers, 12 aides, 2 custodians, 4 cooks, 1 secretary and the principal, Barbara Hood-Winland.

## LIBERTY SCHOOL

Built in 1973 at a cost of $900,000, Liberty School, located just north and east of the Village Mall on Danville's north side, is classified as an open space building—the "classrooms without walls" concept. It has 45,000 square feet of floor space and serves a student population of 375 in kindergarten through grade 5. The staff of 33 has 22 certificated teachers. George Vrentas is principal. The present school replaces the Liberty School which stood for many years at the intersection of Vermilion Street and Liberty Lane.

## DACC STUDENT CENTER

The clock tower adds just the right touch to the Danville Area Community College Student Center; an uninformed observer could easily believe the college was a century old. Actually, the "hallowed halls" impression was ready made for the college which acquired its campus when several buildings that had served the VA Medical Center were declared surplus by the General Services Administration back in the 1960s. The Illinois congressional delegation generally and the late Sen. Paul Douglas in particular worked hard to steer a bill through both the House and Senate aimed at giving these buildings to the college. A fund-raising drive was successful in obtaining nearly a million dollars to renovate and remodel the buildings for college use. Since then, several new buildings have been constructed on campus, the most familiar to the public being the Mary Miller Gymnasium, honoring the late teacher and college president who, more than any other person, brought the institution to life and was responsible for its survival.

## NEW HOME FOR LAURA LEE

On April 26, 1964, a capacity audience jammed the auditorium of the new Laura Lee Fellowship House at 212 E. Williams Street during dedication of the new community recreation center. It was part of the "Bobby Short Day" celebration that also saw about 500 welcome Danville's talented pianist-vocalist at Vermilion County Airport. The spacious building replaces a former private residence that was inadequate and in a state of disrepair. Funds for the new center, which honors the memory of one of the city's great humanitarians, were raised by popular subscription.

'A THING OF BEAUTY...'

The Vermilion Street-Park Mall was a pretty place but decidedly was not "a joy forever." When the first two blocks of N. Vermilion Street, between Redden Square and Harrison Street, were closed to traffic in 1967 and spacious walks, trees, shrubbery, flowers, fountains and sculpture installed, the complaining began. Merchants said loss of vehicular traffic and parking was ruining their business. They finally won their point; the demolition of the mall began in the summer of 1987, with restoration of the street and parking spaces scheduled to be completed by the beginning of the Christmas shopping season.

### SHERATON INN

Filling the gap left by the closing of the Hotel Wolford, the Sheraton Motor Inn at 77 N. Gilbert Street has become luncheon host to many service clubs in its 13-year life. Groundbreaking for the six-story motel was in August, 1972. It opened its doors in January, 1974. There are 114 guest rooms, parking for 150 cars and both a restaurant and lounge. In the early 1980s, a tennis court was built on the north end of the property.

## DOORWAY TO FIRST RADIO

Radio Stations WDAN-AM and WDNL-FM are planning a celebration of their golden jubilee of broadcasting for 1988; it was in the fall of 1938 that WDAN first went on the air. Then as now, the transmission tower, shown above the roof of the studios, was at 1500 N. Washington Avenue. The station, a wholly-owned subsidiary of Northwestern Publishing Company, which published the *Commercial-News*, first had studios in the lower level of the Hotel Wolford. Later the station moved to the second floor of the newspaper building on W. North Street. A group headed by Max Shaffer, long-time station manager, purchased WDAN in 1972 and moved the studios to its present location. Several years later, First Danville Radio, as it was then designated, was purchased by Sangamon Broadcasting Company of Springfield. On August 1, 1987, Sangamon sold to Majac, Inc. Owners and principal officers now are Marc Steenbarger, president and general manager, and his father, Jack Steenbarger, treasurer. The Steenbargers are from Canton, Ohio. WDAN also operated a TV station from 1953 to 1960 when it was sold to Plains Television of Urbana and the call letters were changed to WICD. WDNL has been in existence several years as a companion FM station. There are 30 employees.

## NEW KID ON BLOCK

WIAI-FM is the newest kid on the block among Danville radio stations; it went on the air in March, 1970. Operating on 50,000 watts of power, it broadcasts the Nashville sound of country music 24 hours a day. The station located at 4 N. Vermilion Street in Danville with transmission tower situated near Oakwood, Ill., is owned by Kickapoo Broadcasting, Inc., with Paul Bresee as president and R. Brent Marlin as general manager. There are 17 full-time and eight part-time employees. In photo above, Ken Ball, program director, is at the mike doing a stint as disk jockey.

## THREE DECADES ON THE AIR

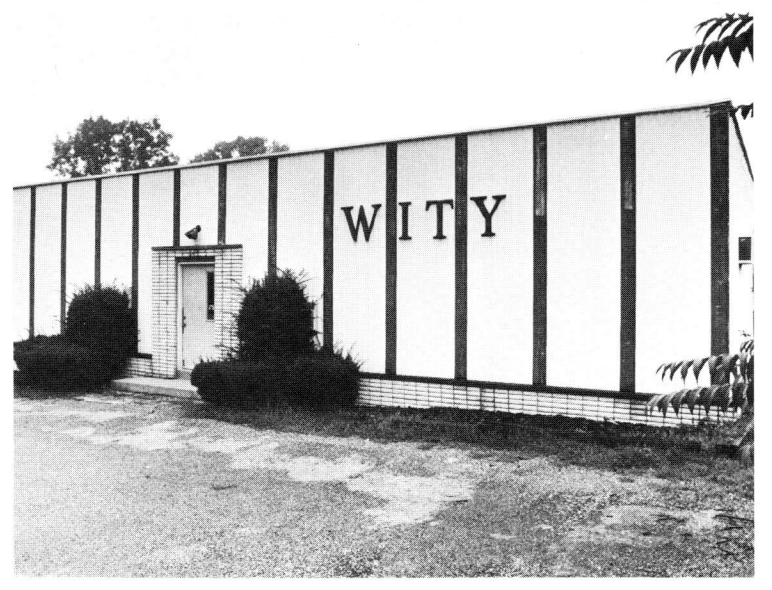

Radio Station WITY-AM first went on the air in November, 1953, and is noted principally for its devotion to sports coverage. For example, it has carried University of Illinois football and basketball games since its inception, also covers Danville and Schlarman High School sports and, at various times, the baseball games of both the Chicago Cubs and Chicago White Sox, currently covering the St. Louis Cardinals. Its unique transmission feature of three, 250-foot-tall directional towers maintains a pattern shape for better day-and-night broadcasting (the station is on the air 24 hours daily). The station provides traditional full service programming with middle-of-the road music. News comes from a local staff and, by satellite, from the ABC Radio news network, the largest in the nation. Present owners are Alan Thomann, president of the corporation and general manager of the station, and Don Ward.

## MUSICALS COME TO DANVILLE

KATHRYN RANDOLPH

Danville Light Opera Company, dedicated to the music theater, has brought a second dimension of the performing arts to Danville since its first show, *The Merry Widow*, was staged April 12, 1956, in the Schlarman High School gymnasium. The organization has staged its productions in many locations-- Danville High School auditorium, the Masonic Temple, Danville Area Community Theater, David S. Palmer Civic Center and the Ramada Inn. First show scheduled for this, the 33rd season, is *The Pirates of Penzance,* the first time ever for a Gilbert and Sullivan operetta in Danville. The first production for the Light Opera's silver anniversary season on September 14-15, 1979, was *West Side Story,* featuring 42 local actors, singers and dancers. Pictured above from that production as the Jets, a New York street gang, are: Front row, from left--Molly Shafer, Tom Ryan, Dale D. Van Duyn and Andy Rennick; back row--Pat Ryan, Jerry Gore, Fred Porcheddu and Steve Hofmann.

IVIED-WALL THEATER

This is the ivied-wall home of Red Mask Players, Danville community theater organization. It is named for Kathryn Randolph, one of the founders of Red Mask, and its only director from 1936 to 1968. Red Mask acquired the building in 1962 from Immanuel Presbyterian Church and converted it into a 225-seat little theater. The organization celebrated 50 years of bringing Broadway plays to Danville (performed by local thespians) in 1986. Two of its illustrious "alumni" are the brothers, Dick and Jerry Van Dyke, stars of stage, screen and television.

179

## SHOW BIZ STARS

A show business columnist once described our city as "Danville, the cradle of the stars."

She mentioned Helen Morgan, the first Danville native to make it big on Broadway and radio and in the movies.

Then she went on to summarize the impact on show business made by Bobby Short, Donald O'Connor, Gene Hackman, Dick Van Dyke and his brother, Jerry Van Dyke. It was an impressive account.

Short is a self-taught pianist of great skill and a song stylist second to none. Numerous show business critics have acclaimed him as the foremost interpreter of Cole Porter songs in the world. He has recorded on the Atlantic label, and has done TV commercials. He once gave a "command" performance for the Duke and Duchess of Windsor in their New York City apartment and has played and sung in the White House.

Bobby started playing the piano for local concerts when he was so young that his feet could not reach the pedals. He was in vaudeville while still just a boy, interrupting the tours to receive his schooling. He wrote a book a few years ago, titled, *Black and White Baby*, telling what it was like to grow up black in a predominantly white small Midwestern city.

As an adult, he is a favorite of Parisian night club fans and has been booked for several seasons as an entertainer in New York's posh Cafe Carlyle, where one of his most loyal fans has been Jackie Kennedy Onassis. He also has been a soloist with the Boston Pops Orchestra.

Donald O'Connor was born in Chicago but has said that Danville is the only home he ever knew while traveling with his

*Donald O'Connor*

*Jerry Van Dyke*

vaudeville troupe family. The Connors of Danville's restaurant and real estate interests are cousins. O'Connor has appeared in many movies, most notably *Singin' in the Rain,* and was the master of TV's *Francis, the Talking Mule.*

Gene Hackman was so shy that he wouldn't try out for a Red Mask Players production while he was working as a cameraman for a TV station in Danville. But he had the acting bug and went to New York City to study. His first break came when he won a part in the Broadway play, *Any Wednesday.* He was a bit player in the movies until he was cast as Clyde Barrow's brother in *Bonnie and Clyde.* In 1971, he hit the top by winning the Academy Award for best actor in *The French Connection.* Since then, he has appeared in many box office hits and is regarded as one of Hollywood's leading actors.

Dick Van Dyke was a $20 a week announcer for Danville's radio station WDAN when he went on the road with Phil Erickson, a high school chum. The two did a comedy routine, lip-syncing to records. He won a contract with CBS to appear on *The Morning Show,* then won a major role in *Bye-Bye, Birdie* on Broadway, a part he also did in the movies. He has appeared in many movies where his best characterization probably was as the chimney sweep in *Mary Poppins* with Julie Andrews. He won several Emmy awards for his leading role in the long-runing TV comedy series, *The Dick Van Dyke Show,* with Mary Tyler Moore. Last Easter (1987), he was featured by Ralph Edwards on the *This Is Your Life* program, emanating from Hollywood.

Jerry Van Dyke, Dick's younger brother, entered show business after winning a world-wide talent contest while serving in the Air Force. He has appeared in several movies, has starred on television and has been featured as a comedian in Las Vegas and in Playboy clubs across the nation.

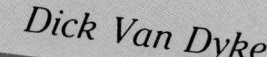

*Bobby Short*

*Gene Hackman*

## CHURCH'S CENTURY-AND-A-HALF

Danville's First Baptist Church dates its beginning to April 12, 1829. The place was the upper story of a frame building on the public square, where Towne Centre is now situated. In 1874, a church building was erected at Madison and Walnut Streets and this served until 1914, when an edifice was constructed in the 400 block of N. Walnut Street, at the junction with W. Williams Street. This served the congregation well for the next 50 years until the present building, costing, $273,939, was dedicated May 3, 1964. In 1973, a church day school of 11,000 square feet was added to the building at a cost of $190,000. A $370,000 gymnasium, attached to the east wall of the school, was dedicated in 1986. The Rev. Harris A. Stuermer has served the church as pastor since 1962.

## ATTRACTIVE DESIGN

The attractive, unusual design of the First Church of the Nazarene at 2212 N. Vermilion Street is evident in this picture of the edifice. The sanctuary has a seating capacity of 675 and the church school can accommodate more than 500. The new church, dedicated July 30, 1972, represents a total investment of more than half a million dollars. The memorial prayer chapel, open daily to the public, is furnished with the original pews and altar from the old church on Franklin Street. The Danville church was organized on March 11, 1912.

## CHURCH AND SCHOOL COMPLEX

The Immanuel Lutheran School, at right above, was built in 1958 and dedicated in 1960. In 1971, it became a unit of Danville Lutheran Schools, sharing educational responsibilities for 240 youngsters with Trinity Lutheran School on this basis: Trinity, kindergarten through fourth grade; Immanuel, fifth through eighth grades. The church, at left, was built in 1971 at a cost of around $450,000 and dedicated in the late summer of 1972. The congregation of 1,667, of whom 1,200 are adults, worships in a sanctuary with a seating capacity of 400.

### SYMBOL OF RE-UNITED PARISH

The modernistic design of the Holy Family Church, located at Main and Park Streets, symbolizes the reunion of the St. Patrick and St. Joseph parishes. Bishop Edward W. O'Rourke of the Peoria Diocese, dedicated the $1.25 million church on November 29, 1981, assisted by the Rev. Robert Hoffman and the Rev. Dennis O'Riley, co-pastors at Holy Family. St. Joseph's parish was founded when German-speaking members of St. Patrick's parish felt the need for their own church, which was completed in 1868. One hundred ten years later, the two congregations reunited, decided on the name, Holy Family Parish, and built the new church. The adjacent parochial school, St. Patrick, also was renamed Holy Family and expanded in size.

### CENTRAL CHRISTIAN CHURCH

The beautiful Central Christian Church, located on the northeast corner of Vermilion and English Streets, and dedicated on December 17, 1950, was the culmination of more than 80 years of worship by this faith in Danville. The Christian Church (Church of Christ) had its beginning here in January, 1868. The first church building was erected at 415 Franklin Street and was dedicated on May 18, 1874 and became known as the "Franklin Street Chapel." Later, after the First Church of Christ at Oak and Seminary Streets was dedicated in 1896, some members wanted a new church in the north part of Danville. They dedicated their new place of worship, identified as the Third Church of Christ, on the southeast corner of Walnut and English Streets. The congregations finally got back together when they consolidated as the Central Christian Chruch in 1928. Plans for the new church home received impetus in 1937, when a fund-raising drive began.

### AWARD-WINNING DESIGN

The triangular-shaped design (to represent the Trinity) of the Covenant Presbyterian Church won the nation's highest professional architectural award for a Danville native, Ray D. Crites, then of Cedar Rapids, Iowa. He was singled out for architectural excellence by the American Institute of Architects. The building, located at the edge of Holiday Square Shopping Plaza, cost $120,000 and was dedicated in 1967. It includes a sanctuary which will seat 200, a kitchen, office, parlor and five church school rooms, The congregation was formed September 10, 1963, with the merger of Northminster and Oaklawn Presbyterian churches. Northminster had been formed in 1961, replacing Immanuel Presbyterian Church at 601 N. Vermilion Street, which dated back to 1881. That congregation sold its building and adjoining manse to Red Mask Players, community dramatic organization, which converted it into a little theater.

## CHRISTIAN SCIENCE CHURCH

Dedication of the new First Church of Christ Scientist at 1400 N. Vermilion Street was on Sunday, September 17, 1980. But services had begun there on May 18, 1969. Why so long between? Because a rule of the faith is that a church may not be dedicated until it is fully paid for. Ralph Bonadurer of Portland, Oregon, was the architect of the church, a replica of one he had designed in Oregon. Cedar from Idaho was used for the exterior and part of the interior. The trim was of heatherstone from Washington and Oregon. The glass windows of many colors are from Kokomo, Indiana. Seating capacity in the sanctuary is about 200. A large Sunday School room and a nursery are included in addition to space for the reading room. The Christian Science religion has been practiced in Danville for approximately a century. The first to study it here were a Mrs. Martha J. Moore, whose sister in Boston, Massachusetts, had experienced a Christian Science healing and a Mrs. Hortense Hamilton who had had a personal healing experience in Kansas City. A Christian Science Society was organized in 1900 and services were held in homes and rented halls until a residence was purchased at 429 N. Walnut Street in 1915 and remodeled for use as a church. The congregation remained there until moving to the present N. Vermilion Street location.

## ROCK CHURCH

Out of a Bible study in 1972 emerged, six years later, Danville's Rock Church, a $1.5-million dollar edifice located on a 12.3 acre site at 20 Poland Road, just east of N. Vermilion Street extended. The sanctuary of the 27,000 square-foot structure can seat up to 1,200, with attendance at present averaging 300 to 350. When a new one is built, the present sanctuary will become a gymnasium. The founding pastors, Paul and Eleanor Stern, remain in 1987, along with associate pastors Bill and Carol Hummer. In addition to starting a church in Rantoul, the Danville church has trained and placed pastoral teams in five churches, supports an evangelist team and teams of missionaries in three foreign countries.

## TENNIS, EVERYONE?

The Danville Tennis Club has been working for many years to make its favorite sport EVERYONE'S favorite sport. A great impetus was given to this goal in 1961 when the first building to house two indoor courts was erected in Lincoln Park. This was the first such facility in Illinois outside Chicago. A second building, also with two courts, was put up in 1977. A clubhouse is attached to one of the buildings, which are heated for wintertime play. The club, which has 240 family memberships, totaling around 400 individuals, supervises play on six outdoor courts in addition to those indoors. Dr. Charles Supple, now of Palm Springs, California, was the chief early fund-raiser. Public donations to build and maintain the club's facilities have totaled between $500,000 and $750,000; among principal donors have been Lou Mervis and the late Howard Lauhoff. Two important tournaments sponsored by the club are one in the winter for boys and girls under 14 and the Western Senior Men's Tourney in the fall. This tournament usually draws 60 to 70 entrants from Illinois, Indiana, Wisconsin, Michigan and Ohio. Tom Simpson, now of Hilton Head, South Carolina, was the first tennis professional, holding the job three years. He was succeeded by his brother, Scott, perennial city men's champion, who has served the past six years.

### SYMBOL OF EXPANSION

Building 98 at the Veterans Administration Medical Center was erected in 1961 at a cost of approximately $4 million. It became the main administration building and had the function of alcohol and drug rehabilitation. Since then, the building has been completely renovated for expanded ambulatory care, a director's suite and beds for rehabilitation and medical patients. By expense contrast, the six-story Building 58, built in 1932 as the main hospital building, cost $1 million.

### ATTRACTIVE CLUBHOUSE

This attractive clubhouse of the Vermilion Hills Country Club replaces one badly damaged by fire in recent years. The club was organized in 1958 when a swimming pool and clubhouse were built. In 1960, a nine-hole golf course was constructed and it is considered by many golfers to be one of the sportiest and toughest in this area. Originally, 89 acres of land was purchased southeast of Danville but approximately a year later, nine more acres were aquired, with an eye to adding nine holes to the golf course at some future date. Currently there are 249 members. The value of the property is approximately a million dollars.

## BUSY AIRPORT

For the size and population of the area served, the Vermilion County Airport is a busy terminal. Started in 1945, it has undergone consistent improvement, including extension of runways, better scheduling of commuter flights, doubling the size of the air terminal building, etc. Continental Express is now the commuter carrier, providing convenient service to Chicago's O'Hare International Airport and connections with major domestic and overseas airlines. A few years ago, the field proper was named Carter Field in honor of the late Clarence Carter, long-time flier and former member of the Vermilion County Airport Authority Board.

## NICE REFLECTION ON LIBRARY

The nearby Wolford Apartments are reflected in the black glass walls enclosing the new rear entrance to the Danville Public Library. The entrance provides convenient access to the building from the parking lot in the rear of the library. New public restrooms were included in the 1979-80 project which cost $110,000. Part of the 1929 brick addition shows to the left of the entrance; the cost of this improvement which greatly enlarged the library's stack space came from the Webster bequest and totaled $8,244. The parking lot is where the old YMCA stood. The library board purchased the building and site for $50,000 in 1972, paid another $28,869 to have the YMCA torn down and prepared the space for parking.

## SAVING AN HISTORIC HOME

In 1982, the Lamon house, built in 1850 and thought to be the oldest surviving frame dwelling in the city, was moved to Lincoln Park from 302 W. North Street, where it had stood for more than a century. It was the home of Joseph and Melissa Beckwith Lamon. Joseph was a cousin of Ward Hill Lamon and had urged the latter to move from Virginia to Danville (where he met Abraham Lincoln and became his local law partner). Melissa was the daughter of Dan Beckwith, for whom Danville is named. One of their daughters was still residing in the house as late as the early 1940s. Money for moving the house and restoring it to its ante-bellum condition came from private gifts, a grant from the Gannett Foundation and from the Gov. Bradford Chapter, Daughters of the American Revolution. DAR members supervised the interior redecoration and the garden clubs of the city took care of the landscaping. The city of Danville gave the Vermilion County Museum Society, owners of the home, a 99-year lease on the grounds. It was opened to the public in 1984.

## DANVILLE POLYCLINIC

In its 40 years of existence, the Danville Polyclinic has become a major factor in the health care services of the community. It was organized in 1947, with the late Dr. Henry Hooker as the moving force behind the project. The location was the building at the corner of North and Walnut Streets, now owned by Danville Township and used for its offices. The Polyclinic moved to its present new 25,000-square-foot facility, a block west of St. Elizabeth Hospital on College Street in 1980, financing the $1.2 million cost with Economic Development Corporation revenue bonds. The staff, which numbered eight physicians in the beginning, grew to 17 by 1986 and an expansion to 44 is considered likely. An urgent care walk-in service was instituted in 1985. A spokesman for the Polyclinic says that a clinic facility to be built in the north end of Danville is being considered. Dr. Muthiah Thangavelu is the present executive head of the Polyclinic.

## SALVATION ARMY'S HOME

The Salvation Army, which celebrated its centennial in Danville in 1987, dedicated its new citadel at 955 E. Fairchild Street on Sunday, October 7, 1979. The Army moved to the new building in August of that year. It had occupied a much smaller facility at 20 N. Walnut Street since 1925. The building, of steel construction, has a day care center licensed for 65 children; a chapel which seats 140; a multi-purpose room and offices; a play area of 7,200 square feet, and parking spaces for 50 cars. Total cost of the project was $500,000, with most of the money coming from a community fund-raising drive. The project included remodeling and expanding a former grocery supermarket for use as the Army's thrift store.

## A BRIGHTER RED CROSS

This October, 1983, photograph shows to great advantage the beautiful new Vermilion County Red Cross building at 320 N. Franklin Street. It replaced the old John L. Tincher home on the same site. That building had been Red Cross headquarters since 1943, when offices were moved from 204 N. Franklin Street. The Tincher home had historical value but was considered beyond repair for practical use. The Red Cross set a fund-raising goal of $350,000 for a new building in 1981, starting with $100,000 from the estate of Ernest and Pearl Jones. The drive was oversubscribed by $17,000. The new building is as utilitarian as it is attractive, providing meeting rooms, storage for equipment and supplies needed to cope with emergencies and space for shelter in disasters. This is the second oldest chartered chapter in Illinois, dating back to 1905. In 1987, the chapter inaugurated a Hall of Fame, honoring those who have contributed greatly to the Red Cross over the years.

## FROM SECOND TO FIRST

Back in 1873, William P. Cannon incorporated the Vermilion County Bank, with offices in the basement of the courthouse. In 1881, the financial institution became the Second National Bank of Danville, a name it would carry for more than a century--until July, 1984, as a matter of fact--when it became the First Midwest Bank/Danville, part of a national bank corporation. With assets of $160 million, it has 98 full-time employees at the central bank, 27 N. Vermilion Street, and at three other facilities: At N. Gilbert and W. North Streets; at N. Vermilion and W. Madison Streets, and at E. Voorhees and Dakota Streets.

## FAVORED LOCATION

The founders of the Palmer Bank back in 1892 would have applauded the choice of their successors in 1976 with respect to a new building: Allowing for changes in street configuration south of the public square, the present-day bank is on the opposite corner of Main Street from the original location. Levin Palmer founded the bank which merged with the American Bank and Trust Company in 1931 and has been known as the Palmer-American since. The cost of the new building, land and equipment was $3 million. There are 36,108 square feet of space on three floors, where 94 full-time employees work. The bank's assets stand at $172.6 million.

## LAKE SHORE NATIONAL BANK

Lake Shore National Bank, 2431 N. Vermilion Street, opened in 1974. Many of the original stockholders also owned shares in the Palmer-American National Bank. In January, 1985, Coyne Richardson of Springfield, who owns nine other banks in Illinois, became the principal owner. Lake Shore has 16 employees, headed by Greg Acton as president and has assets of $18 million.

## BANK OF MANY NAMES

This bank at the corner of Gilbert and North Streets started life in the 1960s as the Bank of Danville. Later it merged with the Second National Bank and changed its name again to First Midwest Bank/Danville when the local institutions became part of a national banking corporation. It functions today as a drive-up facility with indoor services and is the parent bank's consumer finance center.

BACK TO BEGINNINGS

In 1955, the First National Bank sold its "skyscraper" home to Harry "Scotty" McMullen of Danville, who renamed the 12-story building "McMullen Tower." The bank had built this modern-style structure to the west on Main Street, virtually on the site of the first banking venture of Messrs. Tincher and English, the founders of the First back in 1857. When Towne Centre built its office building in the 1980s, the bank leased the entire first floor. The building above was sold to the city which, in turn, made it available to Blue Cross-Blue Shield of Illinois.

HOME--AFTER 130 YEARS

Not far from the humble log cabin of its birth back in 1857 is the elegant building housing the First National Bank, which occupies the entire first floor of the Towne Centre site. The square footage of 23,477 is slightly less than that of the former building on W. Main Street, whence the bank moved in 1984 but usable space actually is greater inasmuch as 15,000 square feet of space was taken up by the bank's computer operation, now housed in a building on W. Fairchild Street. The 1987 assets of the bank stand at $161.8 million and full-time employees number 87. Fancy brick sidewalk in front of the bank's main entrance evoke nostalgic thoughts of earlier bank buildings on the nearby public square.

For the Schlarman High School Hilltoppers, the 1980 football season was very good, indeed. First, they won the Wauseca Conference championship with a perfect 13-0 record. Then they participated in the postseason elimination tournament and emerged undefeated to walk away with the trophy as Class 2-A state champions. Many juniors on that team came back the following year with a 12-1 record but made it back-to-back state title champions in Class 2-A. Squad members pictured above, in no particular order were: Seniors—Brian Henry, Mike Scott, Matt Downey, Jack Whipple, Tim Parr, Bob Robbeloth, David Scott, Jon Cookus, Dan Fredrickson, Chuck Urban; also, Mike Bishop, Steve Fetters, Marty Saucier, Dave Murphy, Kevin Layden, Randy Surina, Jeff Saylor, Mike Carson, Jac Hein, John Altomare; juniors—Joe Berenz, Ronnie West, Jeff Spisok, Dennis Luebbers, Rick Torri, Jim Bishop, Bart Bates, John Andracki, Mark Mayoras, Mike Miller; also, Lonnie West, Tom Vilardo, Dan Dentony, Bill Oreskovich, Greg Robbeloth, Jeff Byerly, Jeff Hein, Mike Spiering, Doug Ahrens, Steve Hirt, Mike Krevalis. Head coach was Greg Colby, with assistants Tom Eder and Larry Baker. Manager was Joe Dunagan. Cheerleaders were Mary Westley, Carolyn Donavan, Beth O'Rourke, Judy Trimble, Staci Hoffman, Theresa Streitz and Cindy Mitchell.

## SCHLARMAN FROM THE AIR

This aerial view of Schlarman High School, taken in 1965, graphically shows the expansion of the facility since 1948. The school held its first classes in the St. Patrick School building (now Holy Family), starting in 1945, then purchased the former Hartshorn mansion at Vermilion Street and Winter Avenue a couple of years later. As seen in the picture, the original home has been added to and a capacious gymnasium built immediately to the west. At extreme left in picture can be seen a part of the gridiron, named Drummy Field for the late Msgr. Drummy, long-time pastor of St. Paul Parish. The school, which accepts students of all faiths, is administered by the Peoria Roman Catholic Diocese. Schlarman itself is named for the late Bishop Joseph Schlarman, who took a special interest in the founding and development of the school.

## NECESSARY FACELIFTING

Old grads deplore the altered appearance but this new addition to the front of Danville High School was deemed essential to educational services. The third floor is devoted entirely to English classrooms, the second to a much larger library and the first to science labs and classrooms. The basement is for art classes, special education classrooms and a teachers lounge. Expansion of bandroom facilities at the rear of the building was included in the project, while a new industrial education complex is in the works. To demonstrate how prices have increased, the new additions, completed in 1974, cost $1.2 million, while the original building was erected in 1923-24 for $1 million.

## GM CENTRAL FOUNDRIES

This aerial view of the General Motors Central Foundry Division plant at Tilton, Illinois, close-in suburb of Danville, shows the tremendous growth of the facility, bell-wether of industrial expansion from the World War II years up to the present day. GM operated a foundry for the Defense Plant Corporation during the war on this site, producing axles for military trucks. After the war, GM built another foundry (shown in above photograph) and produced castings used in GM automobiles. Among these was the housing for the Hydramatic (automatic) transmission. At a cost of several million dollars, GM installed scrubbing equipment on its smokestacks, virtually eliminating atmospheric pollutants. Employment has fluctuated, depending on inventory needs, but has been as high as 2,500.

## FRIENDLY TOWN

Friendly Town was constructed in 1970 in Lincoln Park, with 1971 the first full year of utilizing it to teach children the principles of traffic safety. Law enforcement officers are unanimous in their opinion that its cost of $42,000 was the bargain fo the century. The town duplicates, in miniature, a typical community, with paved streets and sidewalks, a church, school, fire station, etc. Lifelike signals control traffic, provided by the kids (ages 4 to 9) driving tiny battery-powered automobiles. A policeman, "Officer Friendly," supervises the activities and teaches the youngsters how to protect themselves and others from traffic dangers. Private individuals, businesses, service clubs, labor unions and the federal government have contributed to the expense of building the town and maintaining it. The City of Danville, Vermilion County, School District 118, Emergency Services and Disaster Agency (ESDA), the railroads and both the Danville Police and Fire Departments support the program enthusiastically. Since its inception, between 32,000 and 33,000 children have been short-time residents of Friendly Town.

## NEW UNION BUS STATION

This Union Bus Station, located in the unit block of Franklin Street near downtown, was opened in September, 1976. It replaced the one destroyed by fire on June 9 of that year. Two persons died in the fire. The Illini-Swallow Line serves east-west passengers and the Greyhound Line handles the north-south traffic.

## WHERE ELKS GATHER

This handsome structure is the Elks Country Club, located at 332 E. Liberty Lane. It is home to Elks Lodge 332 and its 2,000-plus members, who pledged the money to acquire 192 acres of land near the north edge of the city at a cost of $107,000. Work was started that same year of 1969 on the clubhouse, which was built at a cost of approximately $800,000. An 18-hole golf course was laid out and the first game was played May 29, 1971. The Elks State Golf Tournament was held there in 1987 for the sixth time. In recent years, the club has played host to both the Illinois Junior Amateur Tournament and the Illinois Women's Amateur Tournament. The club has a fine complex of swimming pools. The Elks Blood Bank has its own building on the west side of the property and Lodge 332 recently sold a small acreage which has been turned into a new Liberty Park. Gross investment of the club, including property and equipment, is $2,094,411.

## NEW HOME FOR THE MAILS

This is the new Danville Post Office, started in the autumn of 1984, completed in the spring of 1986 and occupied in June of that year. It faces N. Hazel Street and the building and grounds, including parking spaces for patrons, loading ramps, etc., occupy the entire block bounded on the other three sides by Jackson, Seminary and Madison Streets. The facility, which cost $2.75 million, was built with a projection of the needs and population growth over the next 20 years. The new building has 50 percent more usable space for operations than did the old post office, located on the first floor of the nearby U.S. Courthouse. The present employment level is 113 and the postmaster is David L. Fryer.

## PALMER CIVIC CENTER

In 1976, the Danville Metropolitan Exposition Auditorium and Office Building Authority, a municipal corporation, was formed. This was a big name for a board to allow it to spend big money--$4.6 million to be exact. That was what the new Danville Civic Center cost. Construction was begun in 1978 and on September 6, 1980, the center opened. David S. Palmer was mayor during this period and when he died in office, the City Council voted to name the building the David S. Palmer Civic Center. It has a standard-size ice rink--85 by 185 feet--and can provide portable, insulated floors over the ice for basketball and soccer games. The main arena can seat 4,539. There are smaller rooms for lesser crowds. The center has been home to a semipro hockey team for several seasons and has brought in headliner shows such as the Ice Follies and Holiday on Ice (combined), the Royal Lippizan Stallion Show, Johnny Cash, the Statler Brothers, Charley Pride, the Chicago Symphony Orchestra, Mickey Gilley, the Osmonds and Chuck Mangione. Jim Miles is the center's manager.

The Village Mall, located at Danville's northern edge, is a prime example of rapid mercantile expansion. It began in 1971-72 with the construction of an Ayrway store (now Target) as a northside anchor for the development, with 80,000 square feet of floor space, and a 22,000-square foot National Food Store (now Lowell's). About 1975, the square footage rose to 249,000 with the addition of several shops and the Meis, Inc., anchor store of 50,000 square feet. A large expansion program began in 1984 and on November 8, 1985, the new J.C. Penney Company store, which had been located downtown for many years, opened its doors along with half a dozen shops, adding 60,000 square feet. All this involved the acquisition of Liberty Park (which found a new site on land formerly owned by the Elks Country Club on Liberty Lane) and the site of Recording & Statistical Corporation, which moved to a new building in Eastgate 74 industrial park. On July 15, 1986, a new and much larger Meis, Inc., department store opened and its old location became the site of 16 new shops and a center court. A fourth anchor store was to be announced in the fall of 1987, raising the number of Village Mall establishments to 75 overall, with 500,000 square feet under one roof.

## FAMILY YMCA

Built in 1972 at a cost of $2 million, the Family YMCA's function is just what the name implies: To offer exercise and fitness programs on a family basis, rather than restrict them to boys and men. One of the features of the new building is a huge swimming pool, 75-feet long by 50-feet wide, a change from the traditional "Y" pool of 60 by 40 foot dimensions. The history of the YMCA in Danville goes back to 1883, when meetings were held in churches then in rooms above a store in the unit block of N. Vermilion Street. Summer Bible classes were a popular feature of the early-day YMCA. In 1914, a handsome brick building at the corner of Madison and Hazel Streets became the "Y's" first permanent home. It featured a swimming pool, gymnasium, a bowling alley, steam room and, on the upper floors, a dormitory for single young working men. After the Family YMCA in the 1100 block of N. Vermilion Street was completed, largely through popular subscription in a fund-raising drive, the old building was purchased by the Danville Public Library and torn down to make way for a parking lot for library patrons.

## LATEST IN PRISONS

This is the entrance to the Danville Correctional Center, a high medium security state prison, one of the most modern in the nation. It took nearly two years to build the $40 million facility (including land), which is located just east of the city. There are 14 buildings totaling more than 325,000 square feet. Perimeter security includes a gatehouse, five guard towers, double rows of 12-foot-high chain link fencing topped with razor-sharp concertina wire. Currently (August, 1987) there are 926 inmates, with the average stay of eight months, according to Warden Michael V. Neal. Employment is 323, excluding contractual employees, such as medical and educational staff. This figure is projected to rise to 361. The annual payroll is approximately $7 million, projected to reach approximately $8 million and annual expenditures locally for supplies, ancillary services, etc., is approximately $2 million. Dedication was October 9, 1985, and the first inmates were received the next day.

The Public Safety Building concept was initiated in the late 1960s as an alternative to the aging Vermilion County Jail, which was approaching its 100th anniversary (1974).

During this time, the Danville Police Department was also in need of expanded and modernized facilities.

The idea of combining police agencies into one main facility was a major thrust of the Law Enforcement Assistance Administration (LAA) that was disbursing federal funds to local law enforcement agencies for such purposes.

The planning of the building continued into the early 1970s, with ground-breaking taking place in the spring of 1973. The building was under construction for an extended period of time, due to the default of the general contractor. The building was completed, and occupancy began, in April, 1976.

The 74,000-square-foot structure consists of six levels, two below ground. It was built at a cost of $5.1 million and houses the Danville Police Department, Vermilion County Sheriff's Department, Vermilion County Emergency Services and Disaster Agency (ESDA), Vermilion County Correctional Center (jail) and the offices of the Danville Public Building Commission. It was originally designed to be a twin structure, complemented by a criminal justice complex (courts). That plan was abandoned, however, when funding was not available to build the companion structure. *Caption written by Pat Hartshorn*

The Courthouse Annex is made up of two separate but connected buildings, one formerly known as the Daniel Building and the other as the Milner Building. The former, which faces Redden Square and is directly across Vermilion Street from the Courthouse, was a gift in 1982 from Champaign's Bresee family to the Vermilion County government. The Milner Building was purchased for approximately $80,000.

Renovation costs have been estimated at $1.6 million for the two buildings.

Occupancy began in May, 1986, for the offices of the auditor, the treasurer, the county clerk, the coroner, the recorder of deeds, the supervisor of assessments and the Vermilion County Board chairman. These are all non-court-related offices.

A few years ago, some county offices were moved to the old Vermilion County Nursing Home, located on Catlin Road near Tilton. *Caption written by Pat Hartshorn*

# LEST WE FORGET

This impressive memorial to Vermilion County veterans who gave their lives in the Korean and Vietnam wars was dedicated on May 31, 1986. It is situated on the east side of N. Hazel Street near the intersection with E. Williams Street. The land was donated by E. Robert Pape III. The $100,000 cost of the memorial was defrayed through the collection and sale of aluminum cans and private contributions from individuals and organizations. Members of labor unions, many of them veterans, contributed labor to preparing the site and placing the markers. Although a non-veteran, Harold Leisch of Danville spearheaded the successful effort, assisted by a committee of World War II, Korean and Vietnam war veterans.

## ST. ELIZABETH EXPANDS

In 1958, ground was broken for the new six-story addition. This building provided 211 beds for patients and also included a new kitchen, cafeteria and emergency room. The fifth and sixth floors were not needed at the time, hence were not completed until 1965. The west wing construction cost $10.6 million by the time it was completed. It was opened officially in October, 1983. The addition included the following: Ground floor—Expanded area for physical therapy and occupational therapy; a new loading dock; storeroom, housekeeping, and security department office; first floor—New emergency department; new laboratory area; new lobby; offices for admissions and cashier offices; second floor—New labor and delivery suites; new surgery area and recovery room; doctors' locker room and lounge; a new boiler plant also was built and the old boiler plant torn down. Along with the opening of the west wing, there was a rather extensive remodeling of several areas of the hospital.

## LAKEVIEW ON THE MOVE

The north wing of Lakeview Hospital was opened in 1959, replacing the original building. The name "Lakeview Memorial Hospital" was adopted in 1960. In 1967, a million dollar surgical suite, recovery room and central supply were added. The new $2½-million dollar emergency, out patient and laboratory complex was opened in May, 1976. The name "Lakeview Medical Center" was adopted May 21, 1976. In 1980, Lakeview Medical Center broke ground for a $23.8-million-dollar building program, the most extensive in local history, a combination of new construction and renovation of existing facilities. It included 138,000 square feet of new construction, adding two patient care floors over the 1976 emergency/laboratory wing connected to a four-floor plus sub-basement new wing. An 18-suite medical office building was built just south of the medical center. the Oncology Center of Danville was opened in 1981. This facility, adjacent to the Lakeview campus, was purchased by the medical center for $2.4 million in 1985.

# ACKNOWLEDGMENTS

No historian-author can be satisfied completely with his work. Inevitably, some significant fact has been left out, some important individual has been overlooked, some church, school, public building or business has been omitted.

The author has striven to include as much history, as many pictures, as possible, consistent with the physical limitations of the book. It never was intended to be an in-depth, comprehensive history of Danville with every i dotted, every t crossed. Such a history would require several volumes and possibly triple the number of photographs and sketches contained in this book, which total approximately 350.

Instead, the intent of the book is to present a representative account, through pictures, of how Danville came into being more than 160 years ago, how it developed and grew, what people were like 'way back when, how their life styles changed over the years, how they reacted to wars, to progress, to good times and bad.

In creating the book, through text and pictures, I am indebted to many individuals whose help I gratefully acknowledge.

First of these is my wife, Pauline, who acted as secretary, telephone receptionist, filing clerk and cheer leader. I couldn't have done the work without her.

Next, I appreciate having as backup my advisory committee. I knew the members were there for consultation any time I needed them so my thanks go to Ruth Burcham Howard, Jan Cornelius, Ann Bauer Hillenburg, Bob Shanks, Don Richter and Kevin Cullen. Mrs. Hillenburg, director of the Vermilion County Museum, was very helpful in assisting my search of the photo files of the museum. Kevin wrote the foreword.

Frank "Bud" Cullen's contribution was vital. Already established as a premier historical artist of Vermilion County scenes, his imaginative sketches fill the gap between the beginning of local history and the discovery of photography. In addition, his sketches of Civil War incidents involving Danville men provide a new dimension to them.

Rich Stefaniak, chief photographer of the *Commercial-News,* and Chuck Cannady, staff photographer, took many of the pictures seen in Chapter 5. The chapter could not have been created without their generous and timely assistance.

Many Danville and Danville area residents loaned photographs from their prized personal collections. Their much-appreciated pictures are acknowledged by courtesy lines under each photograph used. Unfortunately, not all pictures could be used. Some lacked quality for successful reproduction; others lacked identifications or dates.

Pictures of the Danville Public Library were provided by David Nolan, a professional photographer and husband of Barbara Nolan, library director. Photographs not specifically identified are from the Vermilion County Museum, the Commercial-News and the author's personal collection.

In general, the cooperation of Danville people in both public and private sectors was wholehearted and complete.

Last but far from least was the invaluable assistance provided by Carol Smock, assistant vice president of marketing for the First National Bank, and Ann McCurdy, marketing staff member. Their help in preparing photo copies was prompt and generous and their willingness to consult the author on ideas for promoting sale of the book is deeply appreciated.

# BIBLIOGRAPHY

Only a few sources were consulted by the author in preparing *Danville: A Pictorial History.*
These include:

Beckwith, Hiram. *The History of Vermilion County.* 1879.
Bowman, W.I. Captions on numerous Bowman photographs.
Bowman, W.I. and Stapp, Katherine. *History Under Our Feet.* 1968.
"Centennial Edition." *Commercial-News.* 1966.
*Heritage Magazine, The.* various issues over many years. Don and Sue Richter, 1987 co-editors and publishers.
"Sesquicentennial Supplement (Danville). *Commercial-News.* 1977.
"Sesquicentennial Supplement (Vermilion County). *Commercial-News.* 1976.
Stapp, Katherine and Sullenberger, Betty. *Footprints in the Sand.* 1975.
Williams, Jack M. *The History of Vermilion County.* 1930.

# INDEX

-A-
100F Building 100
125th Illinois Volunteer Infantry Regiment 33
Acton, Greg 188
Adams Building 66, 95
Aetna House 37
Airdrome 89
Allen Chapel A.M.E. 170
Allen Chapel Methodist Episcopal 42
Allith Prouty Company 93, 109
American Bank & Trust Company 120, 188
American Cancer Society 95
Anchor Hocking 170
Annex Hotel 104
Arlington Hotel 31, 60, 62
Arnholt, Gerald 170
Assembly of God Church 44, 170

-B-
Bailey, Kenneth 165
Baker & Holmes 62
Baldwin, Dr. Herschel 118
Bandy, William M. 35
Bank of Danville 170, 188
Barnum Building 20
Battery A 66, 73, 117
Baum Building 66, 95
Baum Packing Company 168
Beard Ice Company 155
Beard, John 71, 72, 98
Beckwith, C.H. 114
Beckwith, Clarence 52
Beckwith, Dan 7, 25, 30, 186
Beckwith, Dan Bridge 172
Beckwith, Hiram 10, 14, 16, 52, 104
Beethoven Organ Factory 55
Bell, Capt. George R. 33
Belmont Cafe 140
Benjamin Temple of Music 133
Benjamin, Horace 133
Bethel Lutheran Church 138
Big Four Depot 104
Big Four Railroad 38, 104, 158, 163
Bill Unger Harness Shop 62
Billy Noll Sanitary Laundry 124
Black, John C. 32, 34, 81
Black, William P. 32, 34
Blakeney, Hugh 36
Block & Kuhl 158
Bohn 170
Bowman, W.I. "Pop" 113
Bracewell, Bill 126
Bradley, Charles 116, 117
Brand Building 54
Bresee Tower 121, 122
Bresee, Paul 178
Bryan, William Jennings 162
Bryant, R.H. 30
Burton, Capt. Frank 143
Butler, Morton 147

-C-
Calhoun, W.J. 83
Campbell Brothers Packing Company 168
Cannon, Edison schools 128
Cannon, Joseph G. 47, 74, 81, 82, 115, 130, 131
Cannon, William P. 74, 188
Carbon Coal Company 36
Carlton Hotel 96
Carnegie, Andrew 77
Carson Pirie Scott 158
Carter Field 186
Carter, Clarence 150, 186
Carter, Clarence Field 150
Catlin, George 11
Centennial Hotel 31
Central Christian Church 44, 57, 183
Central Fire Station 71, 172
Cessna, Fire Chief Perry 102
Chamber of Commerce 66, 95, 96, 128, 142, 170
Chamber of Commerce Airport 150
Chandler & Donlan 36
Chandler, Col. W.P. 32
Chapman, Robert B. 164
Chicago 38
Chicago & Eastern Illinois Railroad (C&EI) 38, 39, 104, 128, 163
C&EI Railroad Passenger Station 171
C&EI Railroad's Train No. 92 163
C&EI Shops 74, 104
Chief *Keannekeuk* 11
Children's Home 122
Chuckles 128

Church of Jesus Christ of Latter-Day Saints 170
Church of the Holy Trinity 43
Circus Elephants 88
City Hall 66, 71, 102, 172
Clements, Col. 69
Cleveland, President Grover 67
Coffing Hoist 146
Coffing, Fred 146
Commercial Trust & Savings Bank 133
*Commercial-News* 30, 50, 99, 109, 135, 160, 178
Company D 117
Company I 117
Company L 117
Congregation Israel 170
Conley, John 135
Conron, Inc. 106
Consolidated Coal Company 36
Cooke & Hendricks Store 55
Courthouse Annex 122, 140, 194
Covenant Presbyterian Church 183
Cramer, Henry 36
Crites, Ray D. 183
Curtis G. Redden Post 210 Drum and Bugle Corps 159

-D-
D.A.R., Governor Bradford Chapter 97, 148, 186
DACC Student Center 175
*Daily Commercial* 50
*Daily and Weekly News* 50
Dalbey's Restaurant 88
Dallas Bowman Bridge 166
Daniel Building 95, 121, 140
Daniel School Safety Patrol 139
Daniel, A.C. 36
Daniel-Tilton-Grant-Hooton 139
Danville Art League 170
Danville Auto Club 92
Danville Banking and Trust Company 23
Danville Carriage Factory 61, 74
Danville Civic Center 193
*Danville Commercial* 30, 36
Danville Consistory 156
Danville Correctional Center 170, 194
Danville Country Club 109, 136
*Danville Democrat* 30
Danville Dodgers 137
Danville Economic Development Corporation 170
Danville Field 36
Danville Fire Department 30, 143
Danville Firemen 100
Danville Gymnasium 132
Danville High School 52, 53, 179 191
Danville Housing Authority 154
Danville Junction 38, 42, 67, 104
Danville Junior College 57, 127
Danville Light Opera 170, 179
Danville Malleable Iron Company 109
Danville National Bank 123
*Danville News* 30
Danville Plan 128
Danville Police Department 126, 143
Danville Polyclinic 142, 187
Danville Post Office 66, 96, 97, 192
*Danville Press* 30
Danville Public Library 77, 81, 96, 106, 111, 186
*Danville Republican* 30
Danville Stadium 137
Danville Street Railway & Light Company 74, 86, 107
Danville Symphony Orchestra 170
Danville Tennis Club 185
Danville Township 38, 142, 187
Danville Transfer & Storage Company 95
Danville Veterans 137
Danville's Birthday in 1827 12
Danville's First Cycling Club 45
Danville's First Mayor 40
Darrow, Clarence 162
Davis, Judge Oliver 21
DeLuxe Restaurant 160
Denmark 166
Deutsch, Helen 118
Douglas, Senator Paul 68, 175
Douglas, Stephen A. 22
Duke, Olive 118

-E-
ESCO 170
Eastern Illinois Fair 136
Eastgate 74 Industrial Park 193
Economic Development Corporation 187
Elks Club 81, 111

Elks Country Club 111, 192, 193
Ellsworth Coal Company 36
Ellsworth Park 36, 84, 85, 86, 148
Emery Dry Goods Company 95
Engine House No. 1 102
English, Charles L. 57
English, Joseph 51, 56, 189
*Evening Commercial* 50
Everett, Caroline 93
Everett, Fred 93
Everett, Frederich 93
Everett, Fritz 93
Everett, Karl 93
Everett, Otto 93

-F-
F. W. Woolworth 95, 140
Fairchild School 118, 119
Fairhall Elevator Company 148
Fairview Collieries Corporation 167
Faulstich, August 46
Fecker Brewing Company 122
Federal Building 66
Fire Wagons 100
First Automobile in Danville 92
First Baptist Church 44, 182
First Church 17
First Church of Christ 44, 183
First Church of Christ Scientist 184
First Church of the Nazarene 170, 182
First Danville Radio 178
First Mass Transit 60
First Methodist Church 138
First Methodist Episcopal Church 42
First Midwest Bank/Danville 170, 188
First National Bank 31, 51, 53, 60, 62, 64, 66, 71, 121, 122, 132, 133, 170, 189
First Officers 69
First Paving 61
First Presbyterian Church 58
First School 13
Fischer Theater 66, 83, 173
Fithian, Dr. W.E. 10, 22
Force Buggy Company 74
Force Carriage Factory 61
Franciscan Nuns 37
Franklin School 119
Franklin Street Chapel 183
Fred W. Amend Company 128
Free Methodist Church 170
Friendly Town 192
Fryer, David L. 192

-G-
Gallaher's Tik-Tok shop 160
Gannett Foundation 186
Garfield Park 156
Gelman, D.D. 63
General Electric Company 170
General Motors 170
General Motors Central Foundry Division 191
General Services Administration 68
Georgetown Road 94
German United Brethren Church 43
Gilbert Mill 41
Gilbert, Col. Othniel 32
Gillis, Earl 113
Golden Rule Department Store 101
Grab-It-Here Company 149
Grape Creek 36
Graves, Mrs. 36
Great Western 26, 30, 38
Greyhound Lines 128
Grier-Lincoln Hotel 31, 60
Gulick Drug Company 123

-H-
Hackman, Gene 180
Hall, Arthur 78
Hall, Carey B. 95
Hamilton, Mrs. Hortense 184
Harding, President Warren G. 131
Harmattan Mine 167, 168
Harmon, Oscar F. 27, 32, 33
Harrison Park Clubhouse 109
Harrison, John 91, 99, 109
Harwal Hotel 135
Haworth's Smoke House 158
Heath, W.F. 35
Hegeler Sr., Julius 79
Hegeler Zinc Company 79
Heinley's Grand Opera House 60, 63, 66, 83, 173
Herendeen Milling Company & Bakery 155

Hoffman, Rev. Robert 183
Holiday Hilarity 63
Holiday Square 170
Holmes Family 92
Holy Family Church 44, 183
Hope Christian High School 170
Horse and Buggy Days 64
Horse-Powered Ferry 12
Hotel Annex 67
Hotel Wolford 128, 177, 178
Hubbard Gurdon 10, 14, 132
Hulce, Henry 128
Hummer, Bill 184
Hummer, Carol 184
Humrichouse, William R. 164
Hungry Hollow 36
Hyster Company 170

-I-
I & I Swimming Pool 154
Ike Levin's Clothing Store 126
Illini-Swallow Lines 128
Illinois & Indiana (I&I) Fair 136
*Illinois Citizen* 30
Illinois Dept. of Children and Family Services 158
Illinois Hotel 73
Illinois National Guard Armory 149
Illinois Power & Light Company 86, 107, 132
Illinois Printing Company 103, 125
Illinois Terminal Railroad 86, 128, 132, 148, 163
Illinois Traction System 86, 87, 156
Immanuel Lutheran School 182
Immanuel Presbyterian Church 179, 183
*Independent* 30
*Inquirer* 30
Inter-State Water Company 91, 95, 107, 128
Inter-State Water Company Dam 166
International Nursing Home 23
Ira Cronkhite 102
Iroquois Theater Trial 83

-J-
J.C. Penney Company 193
Jackson Wagons 62
Jamison, Cal 89, 153
Jamison, Cal Grocery 153
Jamison, Danny 89
Jenkins Cigar Store 160
Jewell, W.R. 81, 98
Jewell, Whyte Post 728 24
Johnson, Col. R.A. 57
Jones, Bob 170
Jones, Ernest & Pearl 187
Jones, Larry 28
Jones, Lottie 125

-K-
K-mart 170
Keeslar, John W. 83
Kelly, Mike 36, 96, 97
Kenesaw Mountain Landis 137
Kentucky Liquor Store 54
Kickapoo Broadcasting, Inc. 178
Kickapoo State Park 167
Kimbrough, E.R.E. 83
King, Austin 143
Kiningham Boot Shop 160
Kiningham Music Company 133
Kiningham, Ross C. 106
Kirkland, William 36
Kirkpatrick, Robert 10
Klein's Cigar Factory 105
Korean-Vietnam War Memorial 152, 195
Kroger's 149
Kuemmerle's Meat Market 115
Kyger Mill 15

-L-
Lacock, Dudley 36
Lady Cycling Club 76
Lafferty, Mr. 36
Lake Clements 70
Lake Franklin 70
Lake Shore National Bank 170, 188
Lake Vermilion 128, 136
Lakeview Memorial Hospital 66, 91, 92, 195
Laking, Engineer Zack 163
Lamon Beckwith, Melissa 186
Lamon House 186
Lamon, Joseph 25, 186
Lamon, Melissa 25
Lamon, Ward Hill 20, 25, 186

Lauhoff Grain Company 43
Lauhoff, Howard 185
Laura Lee Fellowship House 78, 175
Lee, Elias 78
Lee, Laura 78
Leins Restaurant
Leisch, Harold 195
Lemon, Dr. Theodore 21
Leonard, Peter 36
Letter Carriers 157
Levin, Ike S. 160
Lewis, Allie 118
Lewis, John L. 134
Liberty Park 193
Liberty School 175
Lincoln Hall 31, 58
Lincoln Park 185
Lincoln School 53, 162
Lincoln, Abraham 19, 22, 23, 25, 37, 76
Lincoln, Fairchild schools 128
Lincoln, Robert Todd 131
Lindley, U.S. District Judge Walter C. 137
Livery Stables 70
Logan, Gen John A. 10, 35
Lowe, Shorty 126
Lyric Theater 83

-M-
Maberry, Wayman "Hickey" 116, 117
Majac, Inc. 178
Mann, Joseph B. 66, 81, 83
Marlatt School of Dancing 149
Marlin, R. Brent 178
Masonic Temple 111, 124, 179
Maxwell, Mrs. Disa Jamison 89, 153
McCann, Dr. George 95
McCormack House 18, 31, 60, 62
McDonald, R.D. 195
McKinley School 174
Mckinley, President William 82, 86, 104
McMillan Hat Shop 160
McMillan and Hill 55
Meeks, Frances Pearson 24, 93
Meeks, James A. 24, 93
Meis Bros. Department Store 106, 141
Meis, Inc. 193
Memorial Bridge 72, 148, 165
Mencken, H.L. 162
Mervis, Lou 185
Meyer, Francis J. "Bus" 134
Meyer, Frank P. 134
Meyer, John P.
Miles, Jim 193
Mill Street Bridge 105
Miller, John M. 55
Miller, Mary 175
Millikin Laundry and Dry Cleaners 146
Millikin, Paul 146
Mine Employment 36
Montgomery Elevator Company 55
Montgomery Ward Company 160
Moore, Mrs. Martha J. 184
Moran, Capt. John 32
Morgan, Helen 153, 180
Morris, Lester "Red" 81
Moses, Harry 134
Moses, Robena 134
Moses, Tom 134
Moss Bank Mine 36
Mules and Mud 60
Municipal Parking Garage 172
Municipal Water Sprinkler 146

-N-
Nabisco Corporation 128
National Home for Disabled Volunteer Soldiers 66, 68
New York Central Railroad 128, 163
Newell's Flying Machine 16
Noone, John 68
Norfolk & Southern 26
Norfolk & Western 26
North Fork River 85, 86
North Ridge School 174
North Street Methodist Church 25, 42, 59
Northeast School 174
Northern Cross 26, 30, 38
Northland Christian Church 170
Northminster Presbyterian Church 183
Number of Shipping Mines 36

-O-
O'Conner, Donald 180
O'Riley, Rev. Dennis 183
O'Rourke, Bishop Edward W. 183
Oaklawn 38, 74, 104
Oaklawn Presbyterian Church 183
Oaklawn Shops 163, 173
Oakley Grocery Chain 149
Oakley-Kroger 55
Odd Fellows Building 71
One Hundred Thousand Club 128
Original Plat 12

-P-
Palace Theatre 60, 66
Palmer American National Bank 14, 23, 50, 123, 132, 188
Palmer National Bank 56, 120
Palmer, David S. 193
Palmer, David S. Civic Center 179, 193
Palmer, Levin T. 56, 188
Pape, E. Robert III 195
Parle, Margaret 118
Parrett, William J. 99
Patriot 30
Payne, Lt. Col E.B. 33
Peak Coal Production 67
Pearson, Gustavus 24, 28, 93
Peoria & Eastern Railroad 38, 104, 128
Peterson/Puritan Company 79
Pioneer 26, 38
Pioneer Post Office 13
Pittsburg Plate Glass Company 160
Plains Television 178
Plaster Drug Store 160
Plaut, Mike 161
Plaza Hotel 87, 123
Prairie State 30
Presbyterian Church 42
Price Family 46
Protestant Hospital 66
Public Safety Building 172, 194

-Q-
Quaker Oats 170

-R-
Ramada Inn 179
Randolph, Kathryn 179
Rapson, J.W. Grocery 46
Reason Hooton 23
Recording & Statistical Corporation 193
Red Bridge 15, 41, 72, 165
Red Mask Players 152, 170, 179, 183
Red Seminary 24
Redden Square 14
Redden, Curtis G. 114, 116, 117
Reddy, Joseph 126
Rescue Squad 143
Rhodes-Burford Furniture Store 141
Richardson, Coyne 188
Rieker, Louis Grocery 148
Rock Church 184
Roose, Frank 137
Roosevelt, Teddy 104, 115, 134
Rose Packing Company 168
Roselawn 57
Rotary Club 151
Ruffing, Red 135

-S-
Said, Jessie 118
Salines of the Vermillion 10
Salisbury and Jamison 89
Salisbury, Tom 89
Salvation Army 187
Salvation Army Citadel 71
Samuel, A.R. 137
Sandusky Furniture Store 158
Sangamon Broadcasting Company 178
Sanichas 160
Savoy Hotel 121, 122
Schlarman High School 190
Scopes, John 162
Sears, Roebuck & Company 160
Second Baptist Church 42
Second Church of Christ 170
Second Courthouse 17
Second National Bank 23, 49, 74, 114, 123, 170, 188
Seed, Reva J. 118
Seymour Treat 10
Shaffer, Max 178
Sheraton Motor Inn 177
Short, Bobby 175, 180
Short, John C. 36
Shutts, Loren 45
Simpson, Scott 185
Simpson, Tom 185
Sisters of St. Francis 90
Skadden, Harvey 138
Sloan, Jimmie 134
Smith, Roswell 36
Smith, Sgt. Joseph J. 73
Soldiers Home 68, 69, 74, 137
Spanish-American War 66
Spivey Shoe Store 160
St. Augustine Catholic Church 43
St. Elizabeth Hospital 66, 90, 142, 187, 195
St. James United Methodist Church 42, 138
St. Joseph Parish 183
St. Joseph's Catholic Church 44
St. Patrick Parish 183
St. Patrick's Catholic Church 44, 141
St. Paul Catholic 170
State Line, Indiana 38
Station No. 2 102
Statue of Victory 148
Stephens, Mrs. G. Haven 152
Stern, Eleanor 184
Stern, Paul 184
Stone-Arch Bridge 66, 72
Street Car 74
Strip Bank Mining 36
Strip Mining 36
Stuart-Holmes Shop 39
Stuebe, Albert 115
Stuebe, William 119
Stuermer, Rev. Harris A. 182
Sunday, Billy 75
Supple, Dr. Charles 185

-T-
Taft, Lorado 148
Taylor, Dr. F.W. 43
Taylor, Joseph 164
Tee-Pak 170
Temple Building 66, 95, 160
Terminal Lunch 132
Terrace Theater 55, 89, 149
Thangavelu, Dr. Muthiah 187
The Colony Shop 160
The Dixieland 163
The Interurban 86
Third Church 44
Third Church of Christ 183
Thomann, Alan 178
Thomas Conron Hardware Company 106
Thomas, H.C. 63
Thomas, H.D. 63
Thompson, John R. 79
Three-I League 137
Tilton, Clint C. 98
Tincher & English Store 51
Tincher, John L. 51, 53, 187, 189
Tinchertown 53
Towne Centre 95, 132, 141, 170, 182, 189
Treat Tavern 26
Trent Brothers Lumber and Planing Mill 114
Trinity Lutheran School 182
Truman, Harry 134

-U-
U.S. Courthouse 97, 192
USO Center 56
Union Bus Station 192
Union Seminary 24
United Electric Mine No. 1 167

-V-
VA Medical Center 175, 185
Vacketta, Ore 149
Valmont Electric 170
Van Dyke, Dick 179, 180
Van Dyke, Jerry 179, 180
Vermilion County Airport 150, 175, 186
Vermilion County Airport Authority Board 186
Vermilion County Bank 49, 74, 188
Vermilion County Centennial Celebration 158
Vermilion County Courthouse 49, 59, 110
Vermilion County Farm Bureau 142
Vermilion County Hospital 66
Vermilion County Jail 40
Vermilion County Museum 41
Vermilion County Museum Society 172, 186
Vermilion County Press 30
Vermilion County Protestant Hospital Association 91
Vermilion County Red Cross 187
Vermilion Hills Country Club 185
Vermilion Opera House 50
Vermilion River 41, 87
Vermilion Street-Park Mall 140, 176
Village Mall 193
Vincennes, Indiana 38
Visitors and Convention Bureau 170

-W-
WDAN 159
WDAN-AM 178
WDNL-FM 178
WIAI-FM 178
WICD 178
WITY-AM 178
Wabash Railroad 26, 38, 73, 104, 128, 163
Walgreen Drugs 160
Walker, Mrs. Gladys 153
Ward, Don 178
Washington School 53, 58
Watson 52
Webster Grocer Company 89
Weekly Inquirer 30
West Vermilion Heights 36
Western Brick Company 108
Whyte, William Jewell 116
Willard, Don 93
William L. Davies Packing Company 168
Williams, Amos 8, 10, 26
Williams, Mariah 26
Winslow, Jasper C. 40
Wischer, Rubie 137
Wischer-Roose Field 137
Wolford Apartments 186
Wolford, Capt. Joe 33
Wonderland Park 85
Woodbury Book Company 71, 100
Woodbury Drug Company 23, 123
Woodbury, Dr. W.W.R. 23, 76, 123
Woodbury, Lucy 76
World War I 66
Wortham, C.A. 84
Wyman-Gordon 170

-Y-
YMCA 57, 106, 111, 170, 186, 193
Yeager, Col. Phil 73
Yeomans, Shedd and Leseure Hardware Company 50

199